The Greatest Story Never Told: Returning to the Heart of Biblical Narrative was one of the most enlightening books I've read on how to read and understand the Bible. Enjoyable, readable, and full of those "aha" moments when something often misunderstood becomes clear. I recommend this book for all pastors and followers of Jesus who want to grow in their understanding of Scripture. It should be required reading for every student of the Bible.

Pastor Brian Lavender
Calgary, Alberta, Canada

Dan is a devoted student of Scripture, a dear friend, and a modern-day explorer. In an honest, energetic approach, he invites us to join him on the adventure of laying down filters and norms through which Scripture is viewed and to rediscover tools designed to offer us greater wholeness and understanding of the nature of the Word himself. Steeped in the rabbinic tradition of asking questions, and unafraid of challenge, discomfort, or how the journey may lead away from the familiar and accepted, Dan gives permission to examine Scripture from fresh vantage points, such as overarching themes, "story," and each author's original intent. It is a rare treasure to find a passionate Christ-follower as immersed in Scripture as he is in the quest for exploring and outlining the better narrative, which its closer examination reveals.

The fruit of the journey Dan has undertaken has been personally life giving. Courage, vulnerability, and graciousness have marked his way. His greatest joy is joining other intrepid traveling companions. Maybe one of them is you. "God conceals the revelation of his word in the hiding place of his glory. But the honor of kings is revealed by how they thoroughly search out the deeper meaning of all that God says." (Proverbs 25:2 TPT)

Steven Jones
South Carolina

The Greatest Story Never Told

Dan makes you think. In *The Greatest Story Never Told*, Dan gives those of us who have been taught we only need to let the "professionals" decide what to believe permission and courage to ask deeper questions—the ones no one else is asking or that are deemed too "bad" to ask. More importantly, he invites us into relationship with the living Word. I have never been more excited about reading, studying, and searching Scripture as I am now after reading the truths in his book. I endorse his message fully because, ultimately, I believe this is where we begin to leave behind the pat "answers" that have silenced us and to begin a true journey of discovery of who Jesus is, what he did, and what that means for each of us.

Cameron Jones
Mother of six and passionate Christ-follower

Dan uses his extensive background and expertise to discuss and discern what the Bible is—and just as importantly, what it is not. His insights will improve every Christ-follower's ability to bear witness to our Father's love and his ultimate plan for his kingdom through his Son Jesus.

John Zimmermann
Friend and volunteer advocate for Compassion International

The Greatest Story Never Told:

Returning to the Heart of Biblical Narrative

Daniel Sandler

Cover Design: Vision Tank, UK
Interior Design: Vision Tank, UK

Instagram: @redarrowmedia
Twitter: @RedArrowMedia1
Facebook: redarrowmedia
ISBN: 978-0-9965695-6-9

Printed in the United States
redarrowmedia.com

CONTENTS

ACKNOWLEDGMENTS

Thank you so much, Scott and Marie, for your love and friendship and for inviting me into the vibrant culture you created by teaching others how to hear God's voice. The years you and your amazing kids mentored me were my favorite years in ministry.

Many thanks to Steven and Cameron. You have constantly encouraged me, valued me, and honored me as friend and teacher, calling out the best parts of me that God has formed. You have truly been a catalyst for this book.

This adventure that I am inside of requires traveling companions. Matt and Dixie, you have been so sweet, generous, and intentional about walking this path with us. I am in your debt.

Mom and Dad, thank you for preparing me for life so well, disciplining me to digest the Scriptures in big chunks. Thank you for your pioneering spirit and for teaching me to ask questions and find out for myself.

I wrote this book for my children. I have inherited a narrative from my parents that has been the seed from which my life has grown. I wish to leave the world you are living in with a narrative that more closely reflects the teachings of my rabbi Jesus. Scott, Chris, Cori, Jerry, Ashlee, Jimmy, Bo, Martin, and Akasia, live in God's love, listen for his voice, trust his goodness.

And for my best friend, Karen. Thank you. You've taught me what kindness is. You've slathered my life in grace. You are generous, beautiful, and wise. This book is OUR seed, the result of three decades spent discipling each other and partnering as parents and as pastors.

PROLOGUE

How Not What

This is a different kind of Christian book. I wrote it for everyone, but especially for those who identify as Christ-followers. I use the term *Christ-followers* intentionally to disassociate this book's conversation from what has been accepted as a *Christian* conversation. Many ideas in the current Christian conversation have little or nothing to do with Jesus, the rabbi from Nazareth who lived two thousand years ago. *Christian* has become the identifier for religions, religious values, and church activities that do more to support national, economic, or social agendas than they do to represent Jesus. Being Christian has become entangled with things that I believe confuse the issue and water down the teachings of Christ.

Following Jesus is my endgame. My heart as a pastor is to give people a chance to reconsider how they approach the Bible and derive meaning from it. This book isn't about *what* I believe; it's about *how* I have come to my decisions. I will leave the decision of *what* to believe to you, the reader. My opinions exist in an ocean of other opinions that are claiming "truth" and "accuracy," and I do not wish to be heard on the playing field that I have inherited. Our current "Christian" orthodoxy is a little too sure of itself—I offer my opinions only as illustrations to point toward theological ideas that remain largely unexplored.

The culture of polarizing argument that requires agreement on what we believe in order to stay connected and continue to value each other is one of the main reasons the greatest story ever told sometimes never really gets told. I do not think absolutism (claiming absolute truths), suppositional thinking (converting word pictures and stories into universal principles), or dualism (forcing believers to choose sides) will help us hear the heart of God. I cannot wrap my past journey or your future journey into a neatly defined package. This book is only a beginning. Using tools developed over a lifetime of scriptural study, my goal is to equip readers to think for themselves, discarding the fear of questioning what they have always been told to believe. But before these tools will bear fruit, they must live through seasons of being experienced, inhabited, evaluated, and adjusted to fit. It will take *time*.

But what does time mean to the twenty-first-century mind? We've all heard time can be a tyrant, but for us, time is also a commodity. We celebrate youth and speak of time as something we spend, invest, save, and waste. Time is limited; it's running out. Beyond calendars and clocks, we measure it with the concept of progress. Esteem of progress makes the past depreciated, the present disproportionately important, and the future the fragile offspring of time as a dictator. It leads the value of the elderly to be viewed as diminished, because they have less time, and the young to capture the focus of our attention, because they have more time.

I'm not a fan of this concept of time.

One of the building blocks of my understanding of Scripture is that the ancient world did not perceive of time as we do. Whether because they lacked the science to understand or were more holistic in their thinking, or most likely a combination of the two, scriptural authors and their original hearers and readers conceived of where they fit into history with greater attention to the relationship between the "heavens and the earth" and with less attention paid to the marking of linear time. Their thought process may have been something like this: "Things on earth are the product of decisions made by heavenly beings. We in turn offer our allegiance and worship to the heavenly beings. They in turn respond positively or negatively to our devotion and attention to their values." This cycle helped to establish their place in the world and heavily influenced all facets of ancient society.

Thinking about life and humanity's place in it had cyclical characteristics. This cyclical thinking employed the notion of seasons and respected the movement of birth/spring, growth/summer, harvest/fall, and rest/winter. We see it when the writer of Ecclesiastes 3 tells us that, "To everything there is a season." We see it overtly when Jesus describes God as a gardener pruning those who remain in his Son so they may bear even more fruit (John 15:1–5). Are there any greater examples of patience and respect for seasons than a gardener pruning or the faithful *remaining* and *bearing* (conceiving, being pregnant with, and giving birth to) good fruit? On a larger scale, we see this cyclical pattern in the story of humanity's sin and redemption: God's deliverance of his people from Egypt, from various oppressors in Judges, in the story of Esther, and in a host of other Old Testament books, and ultimately with the sin of Adam and Eve being atoned for by Jesus.

It will be necessary to retrain our minds if we wish to understand the minds and, consequently, the writings of our biblical authors. I believe it is a more effective paradigm to allow revelation to function as a cyclical experience as opposed to a linear one. Instead of reciting what we believe, we are encouraged to recognize the conception of a new idea and to pay close attention to its infancy, deciding how to care for it, examining its characteristics, and intentionally making a place for it in our lives. This intentional space allows us to observe a season of the idea's growth in our thoughts, identities, and choices. Only then will we have a harvest to examine and decide which fruits to eat and which to allow to go to seed for the next planting season. This process is an adventure. It takes effort. It can be exhausting. It needs to be followed by a season of rest.

Thought processes and metanarratives born and raised in this cyclical space, marked by seasons, form beliefs that are not only different in content from those manufactured in the pressure of the now-world of linear time, they allow for them to *function* differently. Instead of contrasting ideas and values meeting on the highway of linear time, demanding an instantaneous answer and resolution to the question of who is "right," we instead have the potential for differing seeds to be sown alongside each other, creating hybrids and cross-pollinating. We have time to watch what grows, pull the weeds, water, and nourish the growth we want, harvest the fruit, take a rest, and try again. We are always learning from the last season and allowing our metanarrative to grow layer upon layer, year after year, season after season—always returning to the exciting, endless possibilities of spring.

This book describes the tools of observing the data of Scripture, living with the unresolved, and understanding the concepts of story, repetition, and author intent. I wish there were a way for me to dissolve chapters and clearly demarcated topics and blend the contents of this entire book into one cyclical but layered experience. How beautiful to allow you to sit in a season of conception and gestation before demanding transition, labor pains, and the birth of new, living values and convictions. But, alas, even the medium of modern book writing is a slave to our concept of time.

However, even within the constructs of chapters and topics, I hope you will allow yourself to approach these tools with a sense of seasons in your heart and to use these tools and this book like a companion on your journey, rather than a source of information to be consumed and then discarded.

But before we begin (just in case you are worried), let me be clear: I love Scripture. It has a story to tell—a compilation of stories, actually, with different facets and perspectives. It waits patiently for one with courage to explore, to challenge the status quo, and to stand face-to-face with the giants of church history and ask one very important question: "Why do we believe that?" There is an adventure of exploration waiting for us in the heart of biblical narrative—the greatest story (n)ever told.

PART 1

CHAPTER 1

THE ADVENTURE OF BIBLICAL EXPLORATION

"We shall not cease from exploration
And the end of all our exploring
Will be to arrive where we started
And know the place for the first time."

—T. S. Eliot, "Little Gidding"

What I am about to share with you is the product of a fifty-year relationship with the Bible. I flat-out love Scripture. My father, from an Orthodox Jewish background, taught me to love it. My mother, of German and English roots, taught me the discipline and the rhythms of structure that would make me a lifelong student of it.

My heritage gave me a unique perspective not only on the Bible but on religious circles in general, as I was prevented from fitting into a cultural box. The Catholic kids in the neighborhood called me Jew-boy, and the Jewish kids shook their heads at the conundrum that was Daniel Sandler: a Jewish kid who didn't go to Hebrew school or synagogue.

Being Jewish meant my father gave us all names from Hebrew Scripture. It meant we were required to know the length and breadth of our namesakes' stories. It meant that we knew the story of Israel backward and forward. It meant that my father thought it was appropriate for a ten-year-old to watch the movie *The Hiding Place*.

Being German and English meant that I had to do something a little different in my heart with the Holocaust and anti-Semitic foreign policies. It meant that I was both a part of the story of Israel and a part of the story of the nations.

Reading and memorizing big chunks of both the Old and New Testament daily made the text of Scripture my constant companion. Sunday school, sermons, and serious conversations ensured that interacting with the meaning and application of Scripture was the foundation of my worldview, my self-talk, and my core values. My childhood made me familiar with Scripture; my faith in God made me love it.

Being a pastor for almost three decades, a father of nine children, and—to date—nine grandchildren, has conditioned my heart to help others grow and find their way. Too often I have watched people curtail their natural curiosity and cease to ask the difficult questions for fear of upsetting the status quo or running afoul of church authority and history. I have stared into the eyes of devastated parents who have been told that their dead children are burning in hell. I have counseled young people who are sure their marriages are ending because God is punishing them for having premarital sex. And I have listened as men and women I respect explain natural disasters and devastating shootings as God's wrath poured out on sinful humanity. As a father and a pastor, I want my children, my congregation, and my readers to feel liberated to look at Scripture anew and be empowered to make their own informed decisions. I want us, as Christ-followers, to reconsider what we believe and, most importantly for this book, *how* we came to believe it.

We have seen what church culture looks like when Christians spend most of their energy fortifying and protecting their existing theologies. Oh, would that we embrace a humbler approach to Scripture and instead of inspiring fear, inspire hope!

I have read and studied history and Scripture extensively, but I acknowledge at the outset that what I am writing is not to compete with the academic works by great minds whose depth of knowledge have influenced me and helped me understand the things I see operating in Scripture. This book is designed to engage the reader in a conversation as to what Scripture is, recognizing that the heavy lifting has been done by others (theologians, translators, archeologists, linguists, etc.). I desire to bridge the gap between the academic works on university syllabi and the more accessible books that occupy the reading tables of the majority of the body of Christ—those who are trying to live like Christ while making their way in a broken world, managing marriages, families, businesses, and personal spiritual journeys.

There are so many places we might choose to begin our adventure of exploration into the story of Scripture. Most of us begin where our fathers and mothers told us to begin. Maybe you were born into a church-going family. Perhaps your first song was "Jesus loves me this I know, for the Bible tells me so." Maybe you learned Sunday school stories from your toddler years on. Regardless of when you picked up the Bible, you have a history with Christian thought and culture. Some of it is definable, like what we were taught from the Bible about the creation of our world or the ultimate destiny of all people to be judged by God and sent to heaven or hell. Some of what we were taught was much more subjective, like who in the church has the greatest value or authority.

From birth until this moment, we have been conditioned to hear or read the Bible a certain way. We have been born into a time and a place where church history has made several huge decisions for us regarding truth, the nature of the Bible, and the narrative of the gospel. We are currently caught in the inertia of theological realities, Christian worldviews, and biblical explanations that flow soundlessly, seamlessly, and powerfully all around us without us even noticing them.

Even more troubling is a concept that can be difficult to process and accept. *All* "truth"—everything we consider to be certain about God, our personal narrative about who we are, and our current understanding of the meaning and intent of Scripture—had a birthplace. At some point in history somebody made a decision about what they thought was true, and then they exercised their authority to teach this truth to others.

It is not an easy thing to admit this to ourselves. It is easier to assume that what we have been taught about God, the Bible, and the afterlife has been taught to us correctly. When we read our Bibles, we come with this assumption. Otherwise, where would we even begin to determine what is true about what we have been told versus what is false?

Make no mistake, like most Christians, I believe with passion that the Bible is a crucial piece of divinely inspired revelation, useful for successfully responding to God and living a life in harmony with his heart. I believe the writings bound in the book we call *Holy* are inspired—breathed out by God through man—and are a master teacher of truth, a primary source of evidence that can produce a life lived from conviction, a wonderful means of allowing God to straighten out our bent lives, and ground zero for effective training in living justly before God and man. In short, I believe that if we commit ourselves to the study and integration of the material in these writings, Holy Spirit[i] will have ample opportunity to grow us into complete Christ-followers, thriving as people whose lives naturally produce the same good works as our rabbi Jesus.

I remember the first time the reality hit me that so much of what I believed had been carefully curated for me, often with an agenda. I was upstairs, studying Scripture as I normally would, when suddenly, I was stunned. There it was, an idea in Scripture that I had never noticed, read about, or even heard before in a sermon. I had been reading my Bible in large chunks for several years, all the while teaching my children and friends in our church the best I knew about what was actually in the Bible.

How could I have been a pastor all these years, the son of a pastor, a Bible college and seminary student, how could I have read the Bible incessantly, book after book, searching honest authors who are writing about their journeys and what they have discovered—and never seen this before?

I will share the actual epiphany later, but perhaps in your own journey through Scripture you have experienced this. To some extent, this kind of revelation is what makes the Bible such a powerful, living, *different* kind of book. And these insights into truth have caused some of the greatest cultural shifts in world history. They have also been the starting point for much division, war, brutality, and pride. The idea that we can understand God, the Creator of the

---

[i] I realize removing "the" from "Holy Spirit" can be distracting, but it is a way to challenge our presuppositions about Scripture and how we interact with it, as I will discuss in more detail later. Is Holy Spirit a person, the same way as Father God or Jesus? I believe "the" depersonalizes Holy Spirit and is a constant reinforcer of bad biblical ideas.

universe, by reading this book is, for some, an absurd concept, and for others, a truth they will build their lives upon. In all cases, however, it is difficult to discern the truth we are receiving versus the ideas, frameworks, and beliefs that we *already believe* before we even sit down to read it.

I used to think that all that was needed to truly understand Scripture was to, well, study it. But I was wrong. Because when those who disciple you decide a good deal of the back story, the core values, and the theological expectations, and then they convince you that these boundary markers are immovable, it becomes inevitable that you will hear the stories of Scripture a certain way. In short, you will hear what you are told to hear. Why is this a problem?

Well . . .

When expectations are more valuable than the skill of observation,

When all the important questions one encounters in the exploration of the stories of Scripture are resolved by systematic answers,

When stories are distilled into suppositions,

When the communication devices of an ancient culture are not valued,

When the intent of the authors is ignored in favor of the chillingly arrogant answer: "Scripture interprets other Scripture,"[ii]

Then . . .

Well, then the exciting adventure of the exploration of who God is and what he is doing on the earth is reduced to a police action, defending stale orthodoxy. The power of the seed of heaven to produce God's image-bearing sons and daughters, who rule and subdue the earth with the DNA of heaven, becomes castrated into the impotence of obedience and fear. The target of our Creator, the purpose for which he made us in his image, is lost in the distraction, hostility, and confusion of factions mutilating each other for the pride of "being right."

So what is my point in bringing this up? To inspire doubt? Fear? To undermine the doctrine of inspiration or somehow dilute the authority of Scripture?

Well, the answer is not a simple yes or no. I do not wish to cause doubt, but I am not afraid to have those difficult conversations that force me to realize that maybe I don't have the right perspective or all of the information or that cause me to take a step back and consider an opinion different than my own.

The process of doubt is not always a destructive one. God called Jeremiah to "tear down" as much as he called him to "build up" (Jer. 1:10 NLT), and in the search for divine truth, especially considering the world we have inherited and live in today, God may require many of our beliefs to be torn down in order that truth—sincere truth found in an honest and humble approach to Scripture—may be built.

What I seek and hope to offer is a more complete understanding of how the Bible works inside its pages. For thousands of years people have paid attention to this odd assortment of smaller writings as if it was something more than a work of literature. Why? How does this book function? How do we honestly approach and honor it? Who gets to decide? Who is the God—the central character—of the Bible? What is God like? Who does this God think we are? Where is it all going? What is God after?

Obviously, none of us can examine these questions in a vacuum. We will

---

ⁱⁱ "Scripture interprets Scripture" is a hermeneutical device employed by the Reformers as a by-product of their reaction to the abusive authority of the pope. Their corrective move was to place Scripture center stage as the sole authority for Christian practice and doctrine. While this was an amazing stride forward, away from human abuses of authority and toward the freedom necessary for individual Christians to interact directly with Scripture, it was not the end of the journey. *Sola Scriptura* or *Scripture Alone* was a useful battle cry as the Reformers stood up to the absolute authority of the pope, but it morphed over the years. As Luther said, "The true rule is this: God's Word shall establish articles of faith, and no one else, not even an angel can do so."

As such, the need to "harmonize" Scripture became more important. This posture accelerated the processes in church history, which solidified many of our unexamined prethoughts. For example: 1) The Bible is one book, and as such should be one harmonious expression of orthodox theology and Christian practice; 2) Where scriptural authors present information that seems contradictory, we begin with the assumption that it is our perspective that imagines the contradiction, not the actual intent of the authors; 3) Where ideas exist in the text that cannot be harmonized with other "more obvious texts," the "stronger" text will interpret the "weaker" text.

I would suggest that these ideas are incompatible with how Jesus related to Scripture. Stronger and weaker are arbitrary evaluations made from a specific culture, from a specific point in history, using a unique set of values that may or may not be similar to that of the authors in question.

need to stop for a second, take a giant step back, and consider where we are in the centuries of theological evolution that have dictated our present understanding of biblical truth. We will need to suspend our need for immediacy, answers, and absolutes, and give this book the time and seasons needed to grow the seed of understanding in our hearts.

What might we discover if we stopped (momentarily) trying to explain things that we only partially understand? What might church culture look like if we stopped (maybe permanently) our apparent insatiable need to fortify and protect our existing theologies? Is it even possible for us to lay down what we expect Scripture to say and examine it again for the first time? Would you be willing to go back to the beginning, posture yourself as if you were an explorer on an adventure into the unknown, as if you were truly *born again*?

As you give yourself to exploring the text of Scripture in large chunks—as whole books and complete literary experiences—you will begin to observe how the minds of those who created Scripture were radically different than the minds of those who are currently attempting to explain it. There is a great chasm between how Moses experienced his world, how he thought, and how he decided what was "true" and how we today experience the world, how we think, and how we decide what is "true." To assume that words written from a culture so fundamentally different from ours can be understood by simply looking up a definition in a lexicon ignores the very important reality that words are informed by the experiences and thought processes of the one who uses them.

So what hope do we have if there is such a great chasm between the authors of Scripture and those of us today who are invested in its interpretation and application? None, if you demand resolved, systematized surety of the meaning of Scripture. Oh, but what an adventure to strike out into the unknown, equipped with honesty, courage, and the Spirit of the living God, to spend eternity on a discovery expedition, growing in knowledge and experience of who God is!

I believe there is a God. *I* will decide what he is like and what my identity is in him. No one else gets to answer that question for me. I want to know what he is doing on the earth and his plan for humanity. I will not be afraid and fall in line behind the inertia of church history. I will not abdicate my identity and ability to live as Jesus lived, because I perceive different stories being told inside the pages of Scripture than the dogma of orthodoxy, which demands absolute obedience.

I am going to read, reread, study, dig, and meditate. *I* am going to sit at the feet of a broad variety of teachers, listen for the voice of the one Jesus promised me, share my thoughts and ideas with my traveling companions, listen to their feedback—good and bad—and finally, go home to my quiet place and answer these questions for myself. I don't think I will arrive at complete answers, at least not in this lifetime. But I'm happy. I'm at peace. I'm living out my faith with my partial answers, my incomplete understanding, and my posture to never doubt that my God is even better than I think.

There has been much written and spoken by others that has been beneficial to my faith, but I refuse to be held hostage by the opinions and theologies of those who teach with such surety, who demand such allegiance to dogmas, and who pollute the greatest story ever told—the heart of the gospel—with fear.

Let me be perfectly clear: I didn't write this book to promote *what* I believe; I wrote it to show *how* I have come to my decisions. It honestly is not my concern or desire for you to agree with my opinions—they are some among many. I only offer them as illustrations of my thought processes and how to use the tools I intend to show you. I want you to decide the *what*. That's really the whole point: As children of God, we are free to prayerfully consider the *what* of Scripture for ourselves. My hope is that the tools I have developed over years of Scripture study will help you do just that.

Consider 1 Corinthians 1:

> I am asking you, my brothers and sisters, because of the values
> we share in our allegiance to Yeshua the King, that you all
> learn to live in harmony with each other. I implore you to learn
> that caring for each other's hearts, honoring each other to the
> point of considering others more important than ourselves,
> and agreeing to remain connected regardless of our differences
> is the cornerstone of Christ-following. I have heard that you
> argue over who has a greater pedigree, those who learned
> from me, those who learned from Apollos, those who learned

from Cephas, or those who learned directly from the King.
This is not how Christ-following works. The greatness of your
pedigree is not what matters. (I am grateful that only a few of
you began your journey with Yeshua through me.) The King
did not send me to collect followers for my ministry. He sent
me to put the power of our King's death on display for you all
to see. (1:10–17, Dan's translation)

But what happens if this new and bold exploration of Scripture leads you
too far from home? Not all are eager for adventure. Some people simply prefer
peaceful, uncomplicated lives and are not quick to go against the grain. Without
obvious evidence of impending disaster, without the chaos and pain of failure,
betrayal, or tragedy, there is no real reason to upset the apple cart, challenge
authority, or go on a risky adventure. Education, money, and health influence
our decision to either dream of adventure or to prefer survival. The person who
can't see where her next meal is coming from is predisposed out of necessity to
hunt for food. The person who has all of his physical needs met has the luxury to
dream about the more.

Culture has a great deal to do with our willingness take risks as well. Our
cultural norms and experiences often dictate the options of our future. Some
cultures value structure and obedience, while others value adventure and
freethinking. But in every human being, regardless of temperament, resources,
and cultural inertia, is that whisper of invitation toward adventure.

But will we listen to it? Between home and our destination lies the journey,
and the journey is filled with the unknown. And let's face it, the unknown can
be terrifying. What if going on this exploration leads us to disagree with our
parents or other family members, change the way we see ourselves, run afoul of
church leadership, challenge long-held assumptions, question the very core of
our existence, and worst of all, fall into heresy and anger God? Maybe it would
be prudent to just stay home, to curl up on the cozy couch of familiarity and
continue numbing the part of our brain that recognizes inconsistencies and
questions the status quo. Home beckons us to stay. Even if my home contains
disappointment and pain, I have constructed a narrative that helps me make

sense of my pain and chosen coping mechanisms to help ameliorate the disappointment. Home is known. Home is easier. Home is safe.

The thing about *home* in Scripture is that God seems to consistently beckon his people away from it. But he always led to a better place through his word and revelation of his goodness. We have to trust him to do that same work in our lives as we step out, as God called Abraham to do one morning, in the direction of the unknown:

> Go from your country and your kindred and your father's
> house to the land that I will show you. And I will make of you a
> great nation, and I will bless you and make your name great, so
> that you will be a blessing. (Gen. 12:1–2)

> Dan's translation:
> I invite you to leave your home, the place you know and
> understand, the only family, identity, values, and culture you
> have ever known. And let's go on an adventure together to a
> land, a purpose, and an identity that I have created just for you.
> I will show you how great you are, how valuable you are to me,
> how crucial you are to the plans of my heart.

So, let's go together on this adventure of exploration. Let's take humility with us and tell Fear he cannot come.

Chapter 2

Examining Prethought

I have nine children. You probably remember that little tidbit from the previous chapter because it is usually a piece of information that people seize upon. Children are a tremendous responsibility and commitment. In our current Western culture, couples who decide to have two or three of these responsibilities are making a "lifestyle choice." Four, five, or six, and people begin to look at you out of the corner of their eyes, waiting for the telltale signs of involuntary muscle spasms or facial twitches. Tell people you have nine kids, and you generally get one of two reactions: eyes glaze over with incomprehension, or words like *crazy*, *insane*, and *birth control* enter the conversation. I get it. It's out of the ordinary. You may have even had a brief moment of wondering if you should trust a guy who makes those kinds of choices.

Even with all the questioning glances, my wife and I view parenting as a privilege. We have some children who carry our physical DNA, and others who do not. They are all ours, and our hearts are full. I will be honest with you, though; there are unique challenges that have come with raising our adopted children. One of the most difficult things for me as a father is to know that my son or daughter had to endure things no child should have to endure. Years of neglect, abuse, trauma, and instability greatly shaped their little lives long before we ever met them. When they entered our home, their way of looking at the world—their paradigm—was set. And frankly, it wasn't very pretty.

A paradigm is the theoretical or philosophical map that helps one make sense of the world. I like to think of it as a camera lens. Though the advance of photo-editing software has greatly influenced what we can do with photography, those who spend much time with the medium will know that the lens still has a tremendous effect on the image. A wide-angle lens can make a room look larger than it really is (Hey! Why are the walls curving?), and a telephoto can make it seem like you are just steps away from a dangerous predator as it devours its prey. Most importantly, however, the quality of lens will determine the quality of the image. If you have a scratched, dirty, or foggy lens, your image will inevitably reflect those imperfections.

Tragically, some of my adopted children, and those whom I have fostered, have had the delicacy of their lenses disregarded. They were scratched, smudged, and tarnished. They were led to believe that is how a lens should be. As a result, everything they viewed and then internalized from the external world was solidified, incorporating all the mess on the lens. My wife and I, with God's grace, have done everything we can to give them a new lens. In some cases we have succeeded replacing the lens, and in others it has been all that we can do to remove some of the smudges. In both circumstances we have had to acknowledge our need for God and his guiding hand. We have had to agree to persevere, even when the task seemed scary and overwhelming.

Imagine a straight line that represents all of the theological decision makers responsible for the unexamined prethought that exists in our present understanding of Scripture—men, mostly, who have made decisions regarding the intent and meaning of Scripture that reflected their own opinions concerning how Scripture works and what they believed it taught.

Why do I tell you about my children? Because I feel that many of us share a remarkably similar experience when it comes to reading Scripture. The lens we were given through which to view these writings has been sold to us as perfect and absolute, all the while ignoring the major blemishes that distort the image. Prominent scratches have drawn our attention, yet we learn to disregard them because we have been raised to accept the obvious inconsistencies as natural, a part of the lens we are just unable to comprehend in our finite abilities. To take a hard look at the lens is disloyal at best and treasonous at worst.

One of the most common marks on our lens is what I call *prethought*.

Prethought is all of the unexamined aspects of our current beliefs about God and the Bible that we bring to the table when approaching Scripture and our relationship with God. They may be accurate, honest, and true—life-giving promises of God's heart for us, or they may be horrible missteps—inaccurate ideas formed from fractured identities, fear-based experiences, or personal agendas. Most likely it is a combination of the two. Prethoughts permeate our experience of Scripture and are the unseen reason our camera lens remains smudged and cracked. They are the birthplace of many of the ideas and concepts that we struggle with as Christ-followers.

Acknowledging prethought is uncomfortable. As I said before, we would like to take for granted that everything we believe is true and taught out of a pure motive. But that simply isn't reality. Our prethought has been formed by people, people who have their own internal narratives, paradigms, core values, identities, and educations. Though they may speak with bravado and certainty, it is strange that we often accept their opinions and ideas without seriously examining them.

Imagine a straight line that represents all of the theological decision makers responsible for the unexamined prethought that exists in our present understanding of Scripture—men, mostly, who have made decisions regarding the intent and meaning of Scripture that reflected their own opinions concerning how Scripture works and what they believed it taught. On one end of the line, place men who did their best to honestly exegete (interpret and explain) the text of Scripture. On the other end, place men who used Scripture to serve their own agendas and values. Every church leader, theologian, preacher, and parent falls somewhere on this continuum.

Even the best-intentioned biblical exegete can make numerous mistakes resulting from the ignorance of ancient culture, worldview, and values. There is great disparity between how the mind of a first-century Jew (or a seventh-century-BC Jew, for that matter) thought and processed his world and how twenty-first-century, European-descended, post-Enlightenment, evangelical minds think and process the world. It is preposterous to read our English Bibles without acknowledging the chasm of evolution between the mind of Paul and the mind of Billy Graham. Language, philosophy, politics, science, morality, theology, and so much more have evolved, layer upon layer, for generations, centuries, and millennia. In light of such difference, it would seem honest exegetical mistakes are inevitable.

And then, of course, there are the biblical exegetes with an agenda. The path biblical understanding has taken down through the centuries has been influenced by politics, economics, the needs of the empire, the need to protect position, power, and possessions, and personal agendas, among others. And so each successive generation has built on the generation before, often without awareness of how the men before them made their decisions regarding the nature and content of Scripture.

Our recognition that it is difficult to know the motives of those who came before us and whose decisions we have inherited is a giant step toward realizing that much is hidden from us in our prethought. Even the construction of the Bible itself is a casualty of the authors' and editors' prethoughts. Let me give you an example. Many of us recall the story of Moses and his encounter with God in the burning bush:

> Then Moses said to God, "If I come to the people of Israel and say to them, 'The God of your fathers has sent me to you,' and they ask me, 'What is his name?' what shall I say to them?" God said to Moses, "I AM WHO I AM." And he said, "Say this to the people of Israel: 'I am has sent me to you.'" (Exod. 3:13–14)

Though scholars do not agree on the spelling and pronunciation of the name Moses heard from the burning bush, it is widely agreed that the Hebrew here should be rendered "I AM THAT I AM" or "I WILL BE WHAT I WILL BE."

This is where God declared his name and how his people were to know the one who would rescue them from slavery, redeem them from fractured hearts, and restore their God-given identities. He was showing *his* identity through his name.

And this is where the seed of one particular prethought begins. For as we read our Hebrew Scriptures in the twenty-first century, we see the capitalized word LORD in our text. Over six thousand times in our Bibles a translator has rendered a Hebrew word that most definitely means something related to the Hebrew verb *to be* as the English word *lord*. As explained in our Bible's introduction, this capitalization of LORD is meant to mark those places where the name of God was originally used in the Hebrew text. But why?

To begin to understand the origin of this change, we have to step back a few thousand years. The Jewish mind was meticulous in its strategizing for how to preserve the Torah, or Law, unbroken. The ancient rabbis built what they called "fences" around the Law with a secondary Law, often referred to as the Oral Law, and this is to what Mark and Matthew are referring when they mention the "traditions of the elders" (Matt. 15:2; Mark 7:3).

Over six thousand times in our Bibles a translator has rendered a Hebrew word that most definitely means something related to the Hebrew verb to be as the English word lord.

This oral tradition was especially important considering most of the populace could not read and didn't have access to written documents even if they could. They depended on the oral teachings of rabbis, and thus the oral teachings themselves grew in stature and power.

A treasure trove of oral tradition and law, providing a glimpse into the thought processes of the ancient Jewish mind, is found in the Mishnah, a gathered history of the oral traditions discussed and taught by important rabbis compiled into one written work around AD 200. In it we find this idea of laws as fences: "The sages said three things . . . 'Be very careful in judgment, raise up many disciples, and make a fence around the Torah'" (Pirkei Avot 1:1).

This Oral Law, this *fence*, was considered as binding as the scriptural Torah, or Law of Moses, and served to protect the Torah from being broken.

Case in point: the third commandment. In Exodus 20:7 the Israelites are commanded not to take the name of God in vain, meaning to use it without a good measure of respect, honesty of heart, and the virtue of allegiance. How were the elders to ensure that people didn't break this command and face the wrath of God? By banning the use of his name in all written or spoken word, that's how. If people couldn't use it, they couldn't abuse it.[i]

---

[i] I deal with the concept and importance of naming in more detail in chapter 7.

While building a fence around the name of God indeed kept the Israelites from breaking the third commandment, I would assert it also had a much more insidious and destructive effect. God called Abraham and Sarah's children to interact with him through the intimacy of his name, invoking the story and the possibilities of a God WHO WILL BE WHO HE WILL BE. Instead, God's chosen people—those he called "beloved" and "firstborn son" and "beautiful daughter"— let fear lead them to avoid his name altogether.

Imagine never using the name of your son or daughter or moving through this life never hearing your own name. What if, instead of calling your spouse "my love," you chose to call him or her "the boss"? Do you think this subtle choice would change the trajectory of your intimacy? The implications for intimacy are staggering—both for families today as well as the people of Israel and their God thousands of years ago. Ponder the effect of this single substitution on the entirety of Scripture. How much of the values, practices, and subsequent theologies of the people of God has been influenced by refusing to call God by his name for fear of breaking the Law?

Can you see the fork in the road where human decision created a reality that, for us, remains unexamined prethought? Here is one example where men made a monumental decision out of fear and became fence builders. That choice of the early generations to avoid the name of God and the intimacy it could have provided formed the prethought of later generations, who in turn made their own choices about Scripture. And because of those human decisions through the centuries, we now have a Bible that six thousand times refers to God as LORD —a name that conjures the English image of authority, submission, and obedience— rather than the pursuing God WHO WILL BE WHO HE WILL BE. Rather than calling God by a name that acknowledges his all-encompassing nature, we have called him something more akin to a feudal lord and overseer. Instead of "my love," we have called him "the boss." That repetition, over thousands of years, has subtly influenced how we view him.

I see this hidden prethought taking shape year after year with my own children. Words I use get repeated, and opinions I have are naturally appropriated and defended without my kids having any real experience or understanding as to why we use a particular word or hold a particular opinion.

Chapter 2

I believe that, as parents, we have to step back and, for the most part, let our children grow and learn at their own pace. Some areas are easier than others, but one arena I usually found entertaining was that of their writing. Children just learning to write and create stories have a method all their own, and it can take quite a bit of work for an adult to decipher the spelling and story line. While I'm a firm believer of helping my children learn and improve and spell words when asked, sometimes it was hard not to step in and fix all the errors—to add my flavor, knowledge, and experience to their work and make it "better."

"You know, if you add a period here, it will make more sense. And these five words are spelled wrong."

"This is a lovely poem. If you would break the lines here and here, it would be even better."

It wasn't that I wanted to hijack their work and make it my own. No, I simply wanted to help them clarify—fix the spelling and punctuation, rearrange it ever so slightly—so that their audience, usually teachers, could understand it better. I didn't want to rewrite anything, so what could be the harm?

But I didn't. Why? Because I wanted it to be an honest representation of what they were capable of, and editing holds power, far more than we often realize. Editors are the hidden hand behind your favorite books and movies, smoothing out the wrinkles, deleting the distracting, focusing your attention. They are a force to be reckoned with because they know even the slightest change can have a tremendous impact. As such, they are given liberty to work their magic.

The Bible is no exception. It too has been touched by editors throughout history.

As best as we can tell, the literary works contained in the Protestant Bible (a distinctly Western tradition) were written between 1400 BC and AD 100. They were written as independent works of literature and, for centuries, existed autonomous of each other as self-contained scrolls or letters. That we approach these individually created literary works as parts of one whole unit overlooks a major component in our examination of this artifact. Enduring decisions have been made by men in authority on the basis of their opinions, and the results are foundation stones to a belief system that we accept as fact because the origins of these decisions are hidden in ages past and are largely left unexamined. To put it another way, as twenty-first century, Western, post-Enlightenment Christ-followers, we are routinely handed in Scripture a laundry list of prethoughts—presuppositions calcified into unexamined, blindly accepted facts.

Consider the answers to the following questions:

- Who determined the order of the books of our Bible?
- Are you aware that the Jewish Bible has a different order than the Christian Bible?
- Is the Bible two halves or one whole?
- Who decided to title the two "halves" the "*Old* Testament" (or covenant) and the "New Testament"?
- Should it be arranged with a space between Malachi and Matthew?
- Is Malachi the last book in Matthew's Hebrew Bible?
- Did Matthew think he was continuing the story of the Hebrew Scriptures and the Hebrew people, or was he intentionally writing the first book of a different covenant, a different people, and a different story?
- Who decided which scrolls to include?
- Why were these scrolls included, and other widely read scrolls excluded?
- Why are there chapter and verse divisions, and who put them there?
- Why are most Bibles filled with extrabiblical paragraph titles informing us of the content of what we are about to read, effectively creating a conscious or subconscious bias toward what we are about to observe?
- Who decided how words should be translated and punctuated in various English translations?

The list goes on, but I believe the point is clear: Internal portions of our Scripture have been affected by external hands. The preconceptions handed to us by others of what the Bible is and is not greatly affect the lens through which we view it, and more likely than not, obscures our view of Jesus, the *living* Word of God, as well.

Remember his words to the Pharisees, those who "knew" from their study of Scripture what their Messiah would be like:

And the Father who sent me has himself borne witness about me. His voice you have never heard, his form you have never seen, and you do not have his word abiding in you, for you do not believe the one whom he has sent. You search the Scriptures because you think that in them you have eternal life; and it is they that bear witness about me, yet you refuse to come to me that you may have life. (John 5:37–40)

In other words, Jesus is saying to these men who have spent their lives contemplating Scripture:

Father God sent me to reveal to you what he is like. You have never heard his voice, you have never seen what he looks like. What he says, what he values, these things have not taken root in you yet. I know this because I stand in front of you as the flesh-and-blood version of his word and his values, and you don't recognize me. You know the Scriptures, what Moses, David, and the prophets have written. And you think their revelation of God is accurate. What you don't understand is that they wrote about God as best they could from their perspectives. Though they peered into the realm of God and saw me, their hearts knew there was more. They hoped for greater clarity and revelation about their God. They longed to see this day. You think that their writings are sufficient revelation to live in the generous love of our Father's lavish heart. Yet, you, the leaders of the people of God, those who know, handle, and teach the Scriptures, refuse to let go of what you think you know and come to me and experience the life you were always intended to live, the life of heaven.

If we want to approach the writings of Scripture in a new way, we must take a hard look at ourselves and our prethoughts. We, like the Pharisees, have to acknowledge and then let go of our hang-ups: our expectations, fears, desires to protect what we already believe, and the preconceived notions and assumptions that have become part of our scriptural paradigm. Even when this task seems scary, overwhelming, or perhaps impossible, we must agree to persevere, acknowledging our need for God and his guiding hand, trusting that he who has started this work in us will be faithful to complete it.

Chapter 3

Authority and Fear

Once one begins to honestly observe, examples of prethought abound. But it isn't always a direct result of something religious leaders have taught or put on Scripture. Repeated behavior of parents, incorporated values from peer groups, trauma, tragedy, joy, success—they all work together to form our personal narrative and affect the lens through which we view the world and Scripture. With such deep personal ties, is it any wonder that we fear to rock the boat and question the paradigm that has subtly been crafted for us by others?

We have been taught to fear subverting the status quo in order to keep the balance of power where the powerful want it. Sadly, a major instigator of this fear in our lives is religion in general, the church specifically. I know this is a bold claim, but the evidence is abundant: Both with great intention and as a by-product, religious institutions throughout the ages have taught us to fear questioning biblical and religious authority. To do so could result in the loss of relationship with friends or family and of our status in community. Even worse, we've been taught to fear our Creator, which calls into question our very eternity!

We know from examples in the Bible that we should submit to authority, but *submitting* to authority has become synonymous with not questioning authority. Why are we afraid to question authority? And, more telling, why does authority get nervous when we question it? Heaven's authority always brings life, empowers, restores, redeems, and recreates. Our Bibles are filled with stories of people who questioned God, as I will share in a moment. He is safe. He is patient. He is kind.

For some, the idea that God is *safe* is hard to swallow. But I would like to suggest that the idea of God being wrathful is rooted in our brokenness, fears, and projection onto God that he behaves as we behave. I do not think God's love for us ever fails. I believe Scripture itself presents the revelations of Jesus as a corrective move toward what God is truly like and away from some of the missteps of those who came before. In other words, our fears of what God is capable of—taught to us through Scriptures that do not include the attitudes, values, or actions of Jesus—are built on the perspective of biblical authors who never met or knew Jesus. These misplaced allegiances have the potential to come crashing down around us if they are exposed for the counterfeits that they are. When we instead put our hope in the scriptural assertion that to see Jesus is to see the Father, we begin to find safety. Others would point to the Old Testament as proof that God is a being whose currency is wrath and fear. I would propose, however, that the journey from the Garden to wide-sweeping narratives of divine wrath, killing, smiting, destroying, and fear involves a good bit of unexamined prethought by our Old Testament authors, who did a good bit of explaining their experiences through human values.

Could it be that the church has picked up a few of the world's tools as it wields authority? Fear, shame, and performance anxiety are not part of God's repertoire. How did they become normal church experiences?

Top-down coercive authority will eventually breed a slave culture where the highest value is obedience. In contrast, heaven's authority looks like the King of Kings removing his outer garment and washing the feet of those who follow him. It breeds trust and partnership and fosters exploration, risk-taking, and creativity.

Those in authority have told us the acceptable versions of the God story and strategically chosen pieces of the story to support their narrative. To question those pieces is to threaten the whole. To threaten the whole is to shake our current expression of Christianity to its very core.

I understand the fear that is produced by stepping out of line and pausing to examine the direction Christians are headed. I understand the courage it takes to put one's hand up to ask, "Why?" or "How do we know that?" or, heaven forbid, "I am not sure I agree with that. Could you please show me your evidence?" Authority is constructed in a very predictable way: Those who have it are afraid of losing it, and those who don't have it are afraid of those who do.

Never was this truer than the season of church history that led up to the Reformation. The pope and his subordinates—cardinals, bishops, and priests—had all the authority: political, financial, moral, military, spiritual, and eternal. The common person, who had none, spent his or her days avoiding and appeasing those who had such pervasive and unrestricted power. But Holy Spirit had a revelation rumbling in the hearts and minds of those who could see beyond the status quo, a revelation that was more congruent with the heart of our Creator, the one who constantly pursues us with love.

Martin Luther said, "A simple layman armed with Scripture is greater than the mightiest pope without it." The Reformers knew that the story of Scripture must be returned to every man and woman, and that the authoritative, coercive, exclusionary posture of many leaders in the church must be protested.

Others would point to the Old Testament as proof that God is a being whose currency is wrath and fear. I would propose, however, that the journey from the Garden to wide-sweeping narratives of divine wrath, killing, smiting, destroying, and fear involves a good bit of unexamined prethought by our Old Testament authors, who did a good bit of explaining their experiences through human values.

Ah, but rarely is a dictator overthrown without eventually being replaced by another. Though the accessibility of Scripture was returned to God's individual sons and daughters in the church, the nature of authority did not change. Fear continues to drive our relationship with authority, and at times even God. We have been taught the Scriptures as a repository of fear-based authority, coercive instructions, and impending punishment. Those who handle Scripture this way insist that Scripture has absolute authority, demand that it be obeyed as a tyrant, and speak of the future with fear and wrath as major players in God's plans to judge the earth. The rest of us are afraid of getting it wrong, because to what damnation could that lead?

What if the authority of Scripture is not a tyrant? What if many of our biblical authors, who never met Jesus, were unaware of what a true servant king would look like? What if Scripture is infused with the authority of a kingdom not of this world? "He who has ears to hear, let him hear" is the Bible's way of saying, "Pay attention to what you think you are hearing. This will reveal to you what is already in your heart."

How does Scripture exercise authority? One observation that grows in stature as I read and reread the Bible is that, internally, authority is presented differently in Scripture than anything I have ever seen in the world of men. I could start with Jesus, but I won't, because it is my observation that Jesus is positioned where he is in the story to restore, redeem, and recreate. Thus, I would expect to find back at the beginning of the story telltale signs of something worth restoring.

Did you know that many of the main characters in the Hebrew Scriptures bargained, debated, and required things of God?

Adam disobeyed God and tried to blame him (Gen. 3:8–12).

Cain killed Abel and complained to God that the consequence was too much to bear, and *God responded with divine protection* (Gen. 4:12–15).

Lamech killed a man and claimed seventy times what God gave Cain. And when the second Lamech was fed up with the curse on the ground, he declared identity and purpose into his son Noah, which means rest, ultimately undoing the curse on the ground (Gen. 4:23–24; 5:28–29).

> *Martin Luther said, "A simple layman armed with Scripture is greater than the mightiest pope without it." The Reformers knew that the story of Scripture must be returned to every man and woman, and that the authoritative, coercive, exclusionary posture of many leaders in the church must be protested.*

Abraham bargained with God over the fate of his nephew in the town of Sodom (Gen. 18:23–33).

Moses argued with God, and God changed his mind (Exod. 32:9–14).

David, after committing adultery and murder, petitioned God for the life of his newborn son (2 Sam. 12:15–23).

Amos, after hearing that disaster was coming upon Israel, interceded on behalf of Israel, and God relented *twice* (Amos 7:1–6).

Jacob, after seeing in a dream a place where angels ascended and descended from the realm of God, a place literally called the house of God, made this if-then deal with God:

"*If* God will be with me and will watch over me on this journey I am taking and will give me food to eat and clothes to wear so that I return safely to my father's household, *then* the LORD will be my God" (Gen. 28:20–21 NIV, emphasis added).

Wow! The nerve! Where does Jacob get this incredible identity? Who taught him to boldly talk to God like this? Why isn't he *afraid*? Imagine Billy Graham giving this altar call: "*If* God provides food and clothes and protects you, *then* ask him to be your God."

There are more examples of those who, when faced with something God said, did not accept it, but rather engaged God with the hope that God would make himself vulnerable to the hearts of his children. Look for them.

What did these men know about how God's authority works that gave them permission to relate to God with such fearlessness, such courage, such expectation? Why weren't they afraid to question the word of God? One direction we might explore to discover new ways of understanding the actions of these men is to realize that they did not have access to the Bible. Their responses and their relationships with God were not filtered and controlled by attention to a book (read: external, codified behavioral rules). The arguing, bargaining, debating, and questioning were the honest and necessary responses of those who saw themselves as valuable, powerful, and important. They believed that God would make himself vulnerable to the concerns of their hearts. Giving away our authority to choose, even to the saints who speak through Scripture, is not how we were intended to live. The Bible, instead of being a repository for the invitation of heaven to live powerfully as image bearers, has become a crutch on which the wounded, disempowered, and fearful of the human world lean for safety.

I would suggest that the world, and not heaven, has crafted a story of God's authority. As such, the building blocks that have been used are tainted by humanity's perspective, a perspective riddled with brokenness, divided hearts, conceit, and self-centered ambitions. The concept of good, healthy authority has been hijacked by centuries of the church wielding the human tools of fear, shame, and performance anxiety to attempt to accomplish heaven's goals.

Many of us will naturally turn to Jesus to find an authentic picture of authority. But we become confused, as we try to plot the posture and teachings of Jesus on our theological maps, by our tendency to view what Jesus does as human, just better—the greatest expression of our concept of authority, justice, or grace as *we* have experienced it. In other words, if Jesus exercises authority, then we expect his expression of authority to be the best version of what we value about authority. It never occurs to us that heaven's authority might be built on values we have never seen before, or more likely, values humanity has forgotten.

But this way lies death. We are blind to our misstep, our misunderstanding of who Jesus is and what and who he is revealing. Jesus is quite clear as he engages the world of first-century Israel: his kingdom—the domain of his kingship, its values, its execution, its very DNA—*is not of this world*. We cannot understand heaven's authority by looking at it through human experiences and imagining the best version of earthly authority.

> For Jews demand signs and Greeks seek wisdom, but we preach Christ crucified, a stumbling block to Jews and folly to Gentiles, but to those who are called, both Jews and Greeks, Christ the power of God and the wisdom of God. For the foolishness of God is wiser than men, and the weakness of God is stronger than men. (1 Cor. 1:22–25)

> Jews demand a sign as proof of authority. Greeks evaluate an idea based on its perceived wisdom. How will they ever embrace the gospel, because our entire story has as its centerpiece *the King dies on a Roman cross*. Jews cannot embrace a king with so little human authority. Greeks will never be persuaded by a story with no perceivable human wisdom. But you and I, brothers, Jews and Greeks alike, know

that our King's story releases the power of God and reveals the wisdom of God to the world. For what the world deems foolish and weak is actually the delivery system for all of heaven's power and wisdom to once again be available to men. (1 Cor. 1:22–25, Dan's translation)

In John 3, Nicodemus came to Jesus in the middle of the night seeking understanding. To this leader of Israel, one who knew the Scriptures and was heavily invested in the current narrative of who God was and what he was doing on the earth, Jesus said, "No one can see the kingdom of God unless they are born again." Leaving aside the important discussion of how an evangelical agenda has forever changed the meaning of this Scripture because of our high-powered priority to get people "saved" or "born again," I would suggest that to comprehend Jesus's words, they would sound something like, "Nicodemus, if you want to understand how my kingdom functions, you will have to lay down everything you believe, everything you have been taught, and the narrative you have constructed from your experiences and *start from the beginning*" (John 3:3, Dan's translation). His kingdom is not of this world!

... the building blocks that have been used are tainted by humanity's perspective, a perspective riddled with brokenness, divided hearts, conceit, and self-centered ambitions. The concept of good, healthy authority has been hijacked by centuries of the church wielding the human tools of fear, shame, and performance anxiety to attempt to accomplish heaven's goals.

To me, this conversation was Jesus telling Nicodemus, "You cannot understand how my authority works by observing how human authority works and imagining the best version of that. In my Father's heart, in heaven's domain, there is a relational pressure, an invitational grace, an opportunity to be who God says you are, without the motivation of anger, fear, or coercive power. Stick with me long enough, and you will see how my response to earthly anger, fear, and coercive power releases heaven's power to restore and give life—a power the world has never seen. Fear and death will be defeated. My kingdom is not of this world."

In Matthew 7:16–20, Jesus also has this to say:

> You will recognize them by their fruits. Are grapes gathered
> from thornbushes, or figs from thistles? So, every healthy
> tree bears good fruit, but the diseased tree bears bad fruit. A
> healthy tree cannot bear bad fruit, nor can a diseased tree bear
> good fruit. Every tree that does not bear good fruit is cut down
> and thrown into the fire. Thus you will recognize them by their
> fruits.

First, this is not a text about eternal destiny. This is a then-unknown rabbi challenging the validity of the authority of the world in which he lives. In his wisdom he asks the question that all healthy authority should welcome: What is being produced by the authority exercised in your life? Good stuff does not come from bad sources. Influence should be judged by what it produces. Healthy authority produces a culture that feeds and nourishes you. Unhealthy authority produces a culture that makes you sick, incomplete, timid, and insecure. Unhealthy authority will not last. Courageous men and women, inspired by God, will question it and partner with God to see this diseased expression of influence come to its inevitable end.

Authority's power to help or hurt people can be scary, but God intends us to be powerful and to wield it. In other words, authority is a permanent God-ordained part of what he wants in his creation. We must learn to steward this authority in a way that is congruent with God's posture toward authority, not man's. We are created by God to subdue it. We must give ourselves permission to judge authority and decide for ourselves its nature, its source, and its fruit.

What is missing from most Christian discussions about community and fellowship is the transparency and vulnerability of assessing the fruit on the tree of authority. This can be especially difficult when the one with authority is someone we love. We were meant for connection. We were designed to be part of something bigger than ourselves. We enjoy the identity and value our primary relationships give us, and the idea of putting these in jeopardy is a non-starter for most people. But fathers, mothers, sisters, brothers, pastors, teachers, and people we respect are all trees bearing fruit in our lives. What kind of trees are they, and what fruit do they produce? What kind of culture do you live in because you stay under the shade of their influence? Are they eager to promote, equip, and champion you? Do they encourage your curiosity, questions, and creative ideas?

It stands to reason that often those who have loved us best and invested greatly in us are most afraid of us leaving them and going on our adventure of discovery. They may push back the hardest. Our parents' narrative should be enough for us. Why aren't we content? How dare we suggest there is more?

I don't mean to demonize those we love. As a parent I can see the natural inclination to feel this way about my own children. After all, I've toiled to arrive at my ideas and beliefs. And since I only want what is best for my children, and no one on earth could possibly love them more, why shouldn't the beliefs I have communicated to them in their best interest stand the test of time and be enough? I get it. But, alas, I am not perfect. My lens has its own scratches and smudges, and as much as it hurts to admit it, I have to acknowledge that some of what I have communicated to my children is flawed. Not only that, but maybe, just maybe, Holy Spirit knows them and their personalities better than I do and has an even clearer way of speaking to their hearts through new and unsettling discoveries in Scripture.

It takes courage, but you are allowed to take the gold given to you by those who raised, mentored, and discipled you and decide that your destiny is further up and farther in. You have permission to choose for yourself how high up the mountain of God you wish to climb.

Will you face obstacles and pain when climbing that mountain? It is likely. Every human being has an instinct to protect those they love. And loved ones will fight against change and conflicting ideas because, in many cases, they fear those changing ideas will bring you harm. They simply can't understand, or they don't want to, and that unwillingness to engage with you in your journey can feel like a prison. I have seen this in my own family.

The Greatest Story Never Told

I grew up in Philadelphia in a community that was part Jewish, part Catholic, and part Protestant. For almost my entire childhood, my Jewish grandmother lived with us. She was Orthodox, which meant she kept all of the kosher dietary laws. Consequently, she had her own kitchen and ate separately from us. But on occasion, the pull of her four grandsons, whom she loved dearly, was too much for her, and "Bubbie" (Yiddish for *grandmother*) would bring her food that she had prepared in her own kitchen, spread tinfoil over the edge of our dining room table, and share a meal with us. (My brothers and I always wondered what part of the Levitical Law expounded on the spiritual properties of Reynold's Wrap that would keep kosher food from becoming unclean.) To the average reader, this may sound unremarkable; however, as is often the case, there is more to the story. I'll have to take you back a few more years to fully reveal the significance of my bubbie's occasional choice to join us for dinner.

My father was raised in an Orthodox Jewish home, which was a culture very different from the average Christian home. The holocaust was current events. Persecution, anti-Semitism, and violence were regular experiences for Jewish people in West Philadelphia. Christianity, as far as my dad's family was concerned, was the religion of Germany, the Catholic Church, and a host of other powerful groups that had persecuted and tried to exterminate Jews.

In short, there was a chasm between my father and the possibility that he might discover the goodness of God revealed in Jesus, the Jewish rabbi from Nazareth. So, what an interesting and unlikely turn of events when my father, at age sixteen, had the most amazing experience with Jesus (we Jews prefer Yeshua or Joshua) and decided that Yeshua was his Jewish Messiah. Did my bubbie and my grandpa sit down with their teenage son and discuss why he had come to this decision, which was counter to four thousand years of family identity? Did they ask probing questions, talk and pray privately, and do their best to understand this radical decision their son had made?

Not a chance . . .

They kicked him out of the house. They told friends and family that their son was dead. My father's own brother, my uncle, stuck a shotgun in my dad's face and told him to stop talking about Jesus. For years my dad was estranged from his family.

He had broken free from their perspective. Because of the culture in which he was raised, he knew his Hebrew Bible (the Old Testament) thoroughly, and that enabled him to see Yeshua in so many Jewish prophecies. He was a man who knew he was responsible to God for his behavior and knew through his Jewish identity that he was chosen to have a unique relationship with his Creator. But rather than live in his family's experience, he stood on the ceiling of the theological house his parents had built and had the courage to strike out in a new direction with considerable opposition.

But somehow, there we sat, decades later, all one big, happy family: me, my parents, brothers, and bubbie, smiling through her tears at the end of the table with her food sitting on tinfoil. Time, necessity, and the gift of grandsons soothed the harshness of her feelings toward my father. My bubbie lived with her "apostate" son for seventeen years. She watched his family's joy, she doted on her grandsons, and she decided that her son had done something right, even though she didn't see eye-to-eye with him about Jesus.

The story gets even better . . .

Every single member of my dad's immediate family—his dad, mom, and two brothers—came to know Yeshua as their Jewish Messiah before they passed away. Our family did not leave Judaism behind; rather, we see our continued journey deeper into the heart of our Creator as the inevitable destiny of the people of God. Yes, our ancestors missed a few opportunities and camped out on the Law of Moses with a fervor that controls and binds us as Jews even to this day. However, the story of Jesus is the aha moment of the Jewish story. God promised to bless the nations through Abraham and his descendants. Jesus is the fulfillment of that promise.

Is there a real reason to fear this journey of exploration into a deeper, more congruent understanding of the story of Scripture? You bet there is. Will you be afraid, rejected, and feel alone? Most likely, at times. But God is better than you think. Perhaps you are the catalyst for taking your family in new life-giving directions. Perhaps your journey will introduce those you love to new possibilities. Perhaps your courage and your faith are all God needs to set those you love free.

Fear of running afoul of authority or jeopardizing our earthly relationships is an effective tool for maintaining the status quo, but the *pièce de résistance*—the tool that has been the most potent in keeping humanity in line throughout the centuries—is fear of our eternal destination. In his frequently referenced sermon, "Sinners in the Hands of an Angry God," Puritan preacher Jonathan Edwards surmises that we are all mere spiders dangling over the fiery pit of hell. One wrong move, and the silken strand is severed by a wrathful Creator, and we are plunged into an eternal suffering that defies imagination. It may sound extreme to put it in such terms, but honest observation reveals that the essence of this message is at the heart of the faith story many of us were told as children. And one need not go back 250 years to hear sermons that communicate the substance of this message: They abound around the world from our pulpits every Sunday.

But it isn't even as simple as choosing God or choosing hell. If one reads between the lines of the prevailing messages out there, even after one has chosen God, he or she walks a tightrope the rest of this earthly life. We are immersed in this message from infancy. You know, to be careful little ears what you hear and little eyes what you see. We are told that getting it right or wrong in this life is how God decides our eternal destiny.

While I realize I have just stumbled onto a topic that will get me vilified as a heretic by some, and I discuss this topic at greater length later, *this isn't a book about hell.* This is a book about how the Bible works and if a new approach to the content of Scripture might produce a different perspective on what God is like. Of course, this begs the vitally important question you will need to consider and decide for yourself: What is the nature of God?

Did the God of the Bible create humanity, fully knowing that many of those who were crafted in his image would spend eternity suffering in torment? Does this suggested narrative agree with what the visible incarnation of God's word—his very heart, his DNA, his only begotten Son—reveals to us? Does this narrative agree with the data of Scripture?

Perhaps our fears concerning the next life are not biblical, but rather a piece of unexamined prethought built by men of fear in a bygone era. You won't know, you can't know, unless you look for yourself. These questions are too important to allow others to answer them for you.

Let me ask a few more questions: Does God love you? Does he like you?

Does God desire intimacy with us? Does God's love pursue you, seek you out, and cherish you, and if so, does he wait for you to agree with him before he does so?

First Corinthians 13:4–8 gives us this beautiful description of love:

> Love is patient and kind; love does not envy or boast; it is not arrogant or rude. It does not insist on its own way; it is not irritable or resentful; it does not rejoice at wrongdoing, but rejoices with the truth. Love bears all things, believes all things, hopes all things, endures all things. Love never ends.

Might I suggest you listen to my wife's paraphrase of these verses as you ponder the concept of God's love in a new light:

Love is patient: God does not expect me to move through any circumstances faster than I can move. He can delay what he wants to give me until I am ready to accept his heart for me.

And kind: He treats me gently, with compassion, wanting to give me the benefit of his presence. God actively looks for ways to draw me closer to him.

Love does not envy: His heart for me is not discontent when I don't respond to Him.

Or boast: He never makes me feel like I am not valued.

It is not arrogant: God has a complete understanding of who he is and his ability to affect my world for good.

Or rude: He is not rough or harsh with me, nor is he crude or imprecise with me. I always know what to expect when he is near.

It does not insist on its own way: God does not make me agree with him. Because he is who he is, he does not crowd the revelation of his love with expectation. He allows me to respond to him in a manner that is consistent with where I am emotionally, spiritually, and mentally, the "who I am" in a given moment or circumstance.

It is not irritable: He is not offended by either my lack of response or the manner in which I respond to him.

Or resentful: God is so interested in my understanding his heart for me that he continually rejoices over me and is in a constant state of invitation toward me. He does not hold my bad behavior over my head.

It does not rejoice in wrongdoing, but rejoices with the truth: He especially gets excited when I receive all that is his creative intent for me. And when my understanding of my identity and his purposes for me collide, he goes off the charts celebrating who I am. He does the Happy Dance!

Love bears all things: My daddy is willing to help me carry all my crap and all my insecurity, and do it so I know it's a joy for him to walk with me.

Believes all things: He knows everything he ever said about me is true and never lets me think that he doesn't believe that I am who he created me to be. Through Jesus he continually intercedes on my behalf to become everything he intends me to be.

Hopes all things: He has an expectation that in the middle of my idolatry, adultery, lying, cheating, laziness, resentment, disbelief, doubt, and running away, that in the middle of everything that pulls me from him, he has a confident expectation that I will turn back to him, because he knows his heart for me is always good.

Endures all things: He will be faithful through all of my arguing, selfishness, offense, materialism, ignorance, ungraciousness, and bad attitudes, because his yoke is easy and his burden is light.

Love never ends: God has never looked for a way to be done with me. He will never look for a way to be done with me.

Sadly, the dynamic between the everyday churchgoer and the holy men (and women) who handle Scripture and teach it from our pulpits is as much a caste system as any fiefdom in medieval Europe. The nobility rule over the common folk with fear and unquestioned authority. The word of the nobleman is worth that of ten common folk.

But . . .

But we are sons and daughters of the King of Kings. We are princes and princesses. We are designed by the one who loves us and crafted us to matter, to speak, and to decide. The slave lives in a culture in which obedience to a higher authority is the highest virtue. What a master says is to be accepted without question and received with that coercive element of fear that motivates a slave to do what he or she is told.

How, then, do we fight such a deep and pervasive culture of fear? We hope. Hope is that wonderful divine residue of our Creator's intent for the absolute goodness of our lives. Consciously or subconsciously we suspect that there is more life to be lived, more love to be experienced, and a more congruent way to live by faith. If fear is the reason to *not* seek adventure, hope is the reason for us to fling ourselves headlong into the expanses of the unknown. Hope conquers fear.

As we go deeper into truth, facing our doubts and fears (and authority figures and loved ones) along the way, hope gives us strength. And our hope is founded in a great promise: Father God and his Son Jesus have sent us a companion, a guide who knows the terrain. We have a counselor who has been this way before, a friend who will comfort, nourish, and encourage us.

> I will ask the Father, and he will give you another Helper, to be with you forever, even the Spirit of truth . . . the Helper, the Holy Spirit, whom the Father will send in my name, he will teach you all things . . . when the Helper comes, whom I will send to you from the Father, the Spirit of truth, who proceeds from the Father, he will bear witness about me. . . . When the Spirit of truth comes, he will guide you into all the truth. (John 14:16–17, 26; 15:26; 16:13)

> Dan's translation:
> I will ask my Father to send you a companion to be with you, one who knows the truth. He will help you and comfort you as you negotiate unknown terrain, cross forbidden mountains, and seek your true identity. The companion I am sending to you will have access to everything you will need for your journey, the entire resources of heaven. Your companion

is a close intimate part of my family, and everything I am, everything I value, and everything I can do will be available to you. I am sending you the most qualified guide, and he will most definitely get you to your destination.

Chapter 4

The Posture of Protection

Prethought and fear are deep grooves in the lens through which many read the Bible, but there is a third deep scratch in our lens, and it is inextricably connected to the first two: protection.

Over the centuries the church has developed a posture of protection. What I mean by *protection* is keeping "dangerously" incongruent ideas, questions, and conversations about the nature of God, humanity, and the gospel out of the hands of the common churchgoer, who wouldn't and couldn't possibly be expected to stay "safe" in such deep theological water. It is this loyalty to protection that has paved the way for the values of perfection, absolute authority, and dogmas to birth schism, divorce, and even violence in the body of Christ.

It is a little known yet fascinating tidbit of church history that in the first centuries our early fathers never endorsed war for any reason. It was not until the fourth century, and the conversion of the Roman emperor Constantine, that we find the authority of human empire joining with the authority of the church. Property, governing positions, tax breaks, and other seemingly valuable items were given to the church in return for assisting in the stabilizing of the empire. This is the point where protection began to pull our gaze off the beautiful wholeness of intimacy with Jesus and his invitation to go into the world to tell people good news about a kingdom not of this world. We, the church, began to read the Bible through the lens of maintaining what the human authority of empire was offering us, rather than following the example of our father of faith, Abraham, and refusing to let any human power be the source or take credit for anything we have available to us in God.

> But Abram said to the king of Sodom, "I have lifted my hand to
> the LORD, God Most High, Possessor of heaven and earth, that
> I would not take a thread or a sandal strap or anything that is
> yours, lest you should say, 'I have made Abram rich.'" (Gen.
> 14:22–23)

We have this tradition of fighting tooth and nail to protect scriptural absolute authority, but can anyone show from the themes of Scripture or our commissioning by Jesus the necessity of adopting this posture of protection?

Take women in leadership, for example. During the middle of a sermon from one of our female elders, we actually had a visiting man get up, interrupt and rebuke her, and call our church out for allowing a woman to have authority and to teach. Why do we feel the need to passionately protect our opinion on what Scripture teaches to the extreme of forcing that opinion on others? When and how did Scripture become so sacred that differing opinions are the catalyst for divorce, hostility, and violence—verbal, emotional, and sometimes even physical?

Please don't misunderstand me: I treasure and esteem Scripture. I study it and incorporate its values into my daily life.

But . . .

I love the Spirit of truth more. When my rabbi intentionally instructs me to look for, receive, and follow one whom he will send, the one who will "guide [us] into all the truth" (John 16:13), then there is only one scriptural thing to be done: We must look for this Spirit of truth promised by Jesus. And we must learn to be guided by the Spirit if we wish to journey into "all the truth."

There is a chasm of difference between something that is true and truth manifested in and through the values and culture of the Holy Spirit of God.

> Now it came to pass, when the time had come for Him
> to be received up, that He steadfastly set His face to go to
> Jerusalem, and sent messengers before His face. And as they
> went, they entered a village of the Samaritans, to prepare for
> Him. But they did not receive Him, because His face was *set* for

the journey to Jerusalem. And when His disciples James and
John saw *this*, they said, "Lord, do You want us to command
fire to come down from heaven and consume them, just as
Elijah did?" But He turned and rebuked them, and said, "You
do not know what manner of spirit you are of. For the Son
of Man did not come to destroy men's lives but to save *them*."
(Luke 9:51–56 NKJV)

The gospel writers have told their stories in such a way to clearly position
Jesus as a prophet like Elijah. Jesus has performed the same supernatural works
as Elijah:

- Raising the dead (1 Kings 17:17–23)
- Multiplying food (1 Kings 17:8–16)
- Exhibiting authority over the natural elements (1 Kings 17:1ff, 18:41–45)
- Meeting with God on a mountain (1 Kings 19:11–13)
- Being taken up to heaven (2 Kings 2:11)
- Placing his spirit on a successor(s), who went on to perform supernatural works (2 Kings 2:9–10)
- Multiplying food (2 Kings 4:1–7)
- Raising the dead (2 Kings 4:18–37)
- Healing leprosy (2 Kings 5:1–14)
- Suspending the properties of water (2 Kings 6:5–7)

It should come as no surprise to the reader of Luke's gospel story that as
Jesus ministered in the power of a prophetic ministry like Elijah's (see Mal. 4:5),
we would see such similarity in the miracles they performed. And since Elijah
and Elisha used their powerful anointing to take life (1 Kings 18:40; 2 Kings 1:9–
12; 2:23–24), it is completely reasonable inside of this very Jewish story (every
Jew knew the stories about Elijah and Elisha) to expect Jesus to call down fire
from heaven, just as Elijah did. But this is where the paths of these two prophetic
ministries diverge. "You do not know what manner of spirit you are of. For the
Son of Man did not come to destroy men's lives but to save *them*" (Luke 9:55–56).

It's hard to miss. *Jesus, although portrayed as having an anointing and ministry similar to Elijah's, is decidedly against taking life.* AND, Jesus ties this dissimilarity to the spirit from which, or through which, he is ministering. The spirit his disciples wish to emulate runs contrary to the Holy Spirit through which Jesus has come to reveal the Father.

I know this observation opens up twenty other questions (see the need for living with the unresolved in the next chapter), but Jesus is pointing us to something crucial that many scriptural exegetes have not sufficiently included in their hermeneutic. The spirit *behind* the truth can actually change the nature and manifestation *of* the truth. Let us be careful what parts of the Bible we submit our lives to. For generations we as Christians have often fought to protect ideas, values, and truths with the wrong spirit.

For protectionism to take root, presumptions have to be made. There are many of these examples of prethought that have worked their way into religious tradition, but following are what I feel to be the main three concerning the nature and authority of Scripture. Examples of these presumptions in use will be delved into further in the "Tools in Action" portion of this book, but I'd like to introduce them here.

Presumption #1: God desires us to have a physical, static expression of truth that we can study to know his will.

Hear the words of Jesus:
"You search the Scriptures because you think that in them you have eternal life; and it is they that bear witness about me, yet you refuse to come to me that you may have life." (John 5:39–40)

And, "I still have many things to say to you, but you cannot bear them now. When the Spirit of truth comes, he will guide you into all the truth, for he will not speak on his own authority, but whatever he hears he will speak, and he will declare to you the things that are to come." (John 16:12–13)

I would propose that in the story of Scripture—from the bad choices made by Israel as they traded in an intimate relationship built on walking with their God by following his spoken word for an external law to be obeyed, all the way through to the revealing of the Word of God that became flesh—we have a clear compass point of God's desire for a person-to-person connection. Humanity, in our God-given intended identity, is meant to know his voice and follow him (John 10:4). This is not static. This is a dynamic, growing, shifting, changing, and living relationship. The mark of a healthy relationship is that it changes and grows. I have yet to see a static relationship that I want to emulate.

Scripture itself is the story of how individuals worked through their own processes of learning to hear and respond to God's voice. Many stories in Scripture give authority, not to a book—a static expression of truth—but rather to a dream, an angel, a prophet, or some other experience that is common to everyman. Looking back at these stories, we imagine that they are unique and unattainable for us today. The truth is, these experiences and others like them, are happening to you every day.

And how are we, fallible beings, to measure the Spirit of truth? Jesus taught us to recognize a tree by its fruit. When we lay aside our obsession with getting things "right," we begin to see that we are invited to observe the measurable harvest of the fruits of the Spirit: love, joy, peace, patience, goodness, kindness, gentleness, faithfulness, and self-control.

> Presumption #2: God allows human history to play out as a product of the free will of man, except when it comes to Scripture. When writing Scripture, God did something different and suspended man's free will to produce an *infallible* and *inerrant* document. In short, Scripture is without error, and is even incapable of having error or leading one to erroneous beliefs. It is the absolute, perfect authority on all matters.

While I understand the reasons and the logical arguments created to undergird such a definition of the nature of Scripture, I wish to point some flaws in the construction of this cornerstone doctrine.

First, I take issue with the idea of a suspended free will ensuring perfect revelation. Scripture records men and women making choices by their free will, without giving us editorial moral evaluations of said choices. We are left to decide what to take away as well as what principle or guidance to derive from each individual story.

Whether it is Terah, leaving the land of his fathers and traveling halfway to the promised land before stopping in Haran (Gen. 11:31–32), or Abraham deciding to have a child with Hagar because the promise had not yet been refined to a child from his wife, Sarah (Gen. 15:1–4), or Jacob and Rebekah's deception of Isaac to obtain Esau's blessing (Gen. 27:1–29), or Moses interceding for Israel

> *For inerrancy, infallibility, and absolute authority to be the guiding values of scriptural interpretation, one must develop these ideas outside of Scripture and then import them into the text.*

and successfully convincing God to change his mind when God declares he is going to destroy Israel and raise up a new nation through Moses (Exod. 32:9–14), or the Spirit of God remaining on Samson despite his wildly sinful life (Judg. 13–16), or Elisha calling two bears down on some youths who were mocking him (2 Kings 2:23–34), or many others, we are given stories in Scripture that have no editorial comments as to the underlying meaning. We are left to our own discernment to decide where God's heart is in the story.

Internally, Scripture does not regularly give us absolutes in the stories where the Holy Spirit interacted with humanity, nor does it give infallibility to the characters in those stories. For inerrancy, infallibility, and absolute authority to be the guiding values of scriptural interpretation, one must develop these ideas outside of Scripture and then import them into the text.

I challenge anyone to produce data from the text of Scripture that asserts that all of Scripture is infallible and inerrant. It simply is not there. No honest exegete will assert that the concepts of infallibility and inerrancy are contained or even suggested by the Greek term translated *inspired* or *God-breathed* from 2 Timothy 3:16. Yet that assumption is the cornerstone of the doctrine of Divine Inspiration.

Frankly, whether or not the Bible is infallible and inerrant is a question not even the Bible would ask of itself. Again, as with the question of eternal destiny,

I often find that people try to answer questions that Scripture isn't even asking or addressing.

Further muddying the waters of our need to protect is our culture. We are westerners, and we value and use absolute authority in a way unlike other parts of the world and other periods in human history. We have been born onto the playing field of right and wrong, insider and outsider, accepted and rejected. We do our politics, our recreation, our conversations, and even our theology as if we were on a football field, each defending our end zones and attempting to take field position from the opposition. A construct that creates polarization, demands that we choose a team, assumes separation from the "enemy," and generally asks us to live outside of the value system we see expressed in the teachings of our great rabbi, Jesus from Nazareth, is not something Christ-followers should blindly embrace.

Absolute authority is such an unexamined part of our prethought that the things I am suggesting may seem ridiculous at first, even heretical. Somehow, the idea that Scripture is perfect, without error and completely authoritative, seems right to us. It's comfortable. It takes the responsibility off us. Somewhere in our spiritual journey someone has convinced us that handing our power to decide for ourselves over to an opinion "greater" than ourselves is the proper posture to protect us from mistakes, otherwise known as sin. The Bible has become the sole repository of authority that governs the ideas, actions, and choices of the Christian. We have pitched our tents under the authoritative covering of infallible and inerrant Scripture, and we censure, and even silence, anyone who would question it.

Where and how does the Holy Spirit, intentionally sent by Jesus to lead us into truth, fit?

What is the nature of truth? Why do we list ideas and doctrines in answer to this question rather than discussing relationships and actions?

If we can conceive of a concept we name *absolute truth*, does it have similar properties to the values, posture, and choices of Jesus—the one sent from heaven to reveal the Father?

Does truth abide in an idea or doctrine, or is truth a person, who lives, chooses, and establishes this thing we call truth?

Presumption #3: Special kinds of humanity were partnered with the Holy Spirit in a unique way to produce revelation that is of a different nature than what is produced through the inspiring work of the Holy Spirit in the lives of Christ-followers today. There are either no longer any humans which are as "special" as the authors of Scripture and/or the Holy Spirit is no longer capable of or interested in inspiring us to produce the same level of infallible and inerrant revelation that we have recorded in Scripture.

Were David, Moses, Samuel, or any other authors of Hebrew Scripture a better form of humanity than we are today? Did God choose a few people for the special assignment of writing the Bible? Was the Holy Spirit inspiration different in the lives of Matthew, John, and Paul than it is today? I realize that you can choose to believe this by faith. I have no problem with the intellectual honesty of saying this

... by the very nature of continued partnership between two distinct beings with different agendas and autonomous wills, it was not long before this God–breathed creation was less than perfect.

is what I choose to believe about the nature of Scripture. I do, however, take great exception to the assertion that what is a faith-based decision is often presented as a fact based on data contained in Scripture.

The concept of God's breath, spirit, and wind is mentioned long before Paul chooses this concept in his letter to Timothy. God breathed life into Adam back in the Garden of Eden. And while I think it is fair to assert that initially this union of humanity and divine breath functioned seamlessly and without flaw, our choice to distance ourselves from our Creator changed the effect of the "God-breathedness" in humanity. God, however, did not choose to take back his image or likeness. God did not choose to "unbreathe" into humanity. He did not separate himself from us nor stop loving us. However, by the very nature of continued partnership between two distinct beings with different agendas and autonomous wills, it was not long before this God–breathed creation was less than perfect.

This concept of "God-breathed" functions similarly in the writing of God literature as it does in the creation of God beings. The partnership implies two distinct forces at work: one holy and whole in every way, the other carrying the image of the one who is whole yet autonomous and often thinks, acts, and speaks from a fractured identity.

Nonetheless, God has chosen to hitch his wagon to humanity.

He has always wanted a powerful force standing face-to-face with Him. He has always intended to rule and subdue the earth and cover it with his glory through humanity. He has never given up on us, despite the weakness of our character, the horrible choices of our will, and the fear that we will never again be significant.

Like the rabbis of old, we have built fences to keep error out. The unintended consequence of building those fences is that we have incarcerated the church in a smaller kingdom and identity than our Creator intends for us to occupy. If God confidently placed two trees in the Garden of intimacy with him, and humanity chose wrongly; if God chose Abraham and his descendants to bless the nations, and they seem to have lost their true identity; if the one like a Son of Man can lose his religious and political fight on a Roman cross, and *still* God gets his way, then I would like to make a suggestion: We should start trusting God's ability to accomplish his purposes his way and stop trying to help him with ideas that run counter to his incredibly creative, gracious, and hope-filled heart!

We are at a crossroads. We have a choice to make. Is study of the Bible a journey of exploration and discovery, or is it a police action designed to keep a tyrant in power? Is the tone of our approach to Scripture protection, or is it creativity? Is faith about knowing the right answer to the question and living cookie-cutter lives under the authoritative doctrinal decisions of others, or is faith *not* knowing yet exploring, hoping, and pursuing greater understanding?

It is time for us as individual sons and daughters to take back the final say of how Scripture works and what it teaches us from the protectors of orthodoxy. *God-breathed Scripture will require God-breathed interpretation.* We must allow Scripture itself, through the leading of the Holy Spirit, to teach us what it is and how it functions, and examine every doctrine, idea, and piece of our Christ-following narrative without fear.

Chapter 5

The Tools

It is said that a craftsman is only as good as his or her tools. In my experience I have found this largely to be true. My boys were always trying to build things out of my scrap lumber in the shop. They loved to use my handsaw and cut boards and nail them together into various boxes of different shapes and sizes. Projects that took them hours would one day take ten minutes with the proper tools. And, quite frankly, the results would be noticeably better.

One of my all-time favorite tools is a six-foot piece of garden hose. This unseemly tool found its way into my life and heart twenty years ago when my wife and I bought a transportation business. I had left the city of my youth and been pastoring in Montana for several years by this time. We started the business small, with just two diesel trucks, no employees, and my wife and I the only drivers.

I always had a lot on my mind as I navigated my responsibilities as both a truck driver and a pastor, and as my deliveries were drawing to a close one day, I pulled into a gas station and did what I had mindlessly done for more than a decade—pumped gas. Unremarkable, I know. What made this time just a bit different was that I distractedly filled my truck's diesel tank with forty gallons of unleaded gasoline. Those who aren't cringing right now don't know that unleaded gasoline will ruin a diesel engine.

I realized with a shock what a huge mistake I had made and quickly did the math: the cost of a tow truck, removing, draining, and reinstalling various parts, plus the wages lost while the truck was out of use equaled well over a thousand dollars. This wasn't good. Frantically, I phoned a friend and told him what I had done. Ten minutes later he showed up with five gas cans and a six-foot length of garden hose.

I was a bit perplexed as my friend put one end of the hose in the fuel tank, and the other to his lips. Having grown up in the city, I had read and heard about *siphoning* and thought I knew what it meant, but in my mind it involved a vague notion of puncturing a hole through the bottom of the gas tank. To be honest, I didn't even know liquid could run uphill against gravity because of how air pressure works, or that a six-foot length of garden hose, as long as it stayed full and the open end stayed lower than the end in the fuel tank, would continue to carry the fuel up out of the tank and then down into the gas cans. Brilliant! I had seen the word *siphoning* dozens of times in books and had created a concept that I believed this word represented. However, I had never actually seen a person siphoning and was victim to one of life's most common blind spots: I didn't know what I didn't know. In creating a definition for a word with which I had no first-hand experience, I had locked myself out of benefitting from this simple six-foot length of hose. I was anxiously counting hundreds of dollars of lost revenue while my friend was calmly using a two-dollar tool. This unassuming garden hose had saved me a day's lost wages and a thousand dollars. Who knew?

It is precisely because tools are so important that I feel compelled to share with you the ones that I have found effective in the study of Scripture. Over the years, I've experienced a great deal of pushback when offering my theological opinions. Very few, if any, of my conversation partners are handling the Scriptures with the same exegetical tools I use. Not only are the tools different, but their approach to *using* their tools of choice is in stark contrast and often with a slightly different end in mind. I am in no way saying that other believers are not also searching for a deeper understanding of and relationship with God through the study of Scripture. But many often want concrete answers, and they want them *now*. But in the intensity of our need to have correct theology and to believe rightly now, we often miss out on experiences that would inform and influence the same theology and belief we so desperately want to get "right."

Honestly, I believe that summarizing the tools before I start showing you the process puts the cart before the horse. However, my experience is that this examination of how we think has proven to be counterintuitive to so many people that I am compelled to give you a map of the tools before we put them into action.

Tool #1: Observation

Think of observation as the first tool in your hermeneutical tool belt.[i] Any
   honest intellectual process of forming an opinion concerning the
   intended meaning of Scripture must begin with observation. Honesty
   demands that we not predetermine what Scripture is and then read it
   through those predetermined ideas. We will never see anything other
   than what we are told to see (or want to see) unless we practice this skill.
   Scripture is something intentional. The surest path toward discovery
   of its nature and its significance is *observing* and interacting with its
   contents.

Observation + Historical Information	=	A greater chance to hear the author's original intent

As we dig deeper into the tool of observation, it is necessary to establish
what I mean by the term *data*. The dictionary defines *data* as "factual
information (such as measurements or statistics) used as a basis for reasoning,
discussion, or calculation."[1] Data is observable pieces of information that are
asserted by the author. Data is not interpretation, and it is not opinion—opinion
is the hypothesis we construct with the data.

A detective observes details of a crime scene and forms an opinion that
includes as much data as possible and then sets off to either confirm or disprove
that opinion. The ability to observe data well can almost be considered a
superpower—just look at Sherlock Holmes. But while data can be interpreted
differently by different people, the data itself remains constant. As I have said
before, nowhere in this book will I tell you what to believe about a particular
Scripture passage. I will report the data and give you my *opinion* as to the
direction my observations point, but you are free to do what you will with my

---

[i] Hermeneutics is defined as the theory and methodology of interpretation, especially of
scriptural text.

opinions. However, the data remains the data.

Let me use another example. Suppose we see a large Down Syndrome man picking up a baby. Even the most gracious, understanding souls in the country might fear for the child and struggle with the appropriate way to react. The data at their disposal is meager, and what they know of Down Syndrome is primarily negative.

But my reaction is different because I have a more extensive collection of data on which I form my opinion. My son has Down Syndrome, and I have seen him pick up babies hundreds of times. I know that in my son's arms is one of the safest places that baby will ever be. I don't blame those with less data for coming to the conclusions they do, but it would be irresponsible, and just flat-out stubborn, to insist on maintaining a position once contradicting data is introduced into the situation.

There is another lesson that my son can teach us about observation, and it echoes with the call of Jesus to emulate children. I have watched countless times as people encounter my son, and what I observe is fascinating. Almost all children are drawn to him. He is different, but he is also utterly joyful and at peace, willing to smile. He is an oversized boy, yet he is eager to pay attention to a smaller child, and it intrigues them. After observing him, many of these children choose to engage with him. Many adults, however, see my son, smile knowingly at me, and then continue on their way without engaging. Now, I realize that most adults have tighter schedules than children and there is a practical reason to not stop and respond to my son's smile, and perhaps they just aren't sure of the appropriate way to respond. But I often wonder if the adult observation and subsequent response to my son is a result of the data they have about Down Syndrome, and it causes them to see what they expect to see. They aren't looking for anything from this young man. After all, he is obviously handicapped, different, and needs to be cared for by special people who understand his condition.

What uninformed children notice that well-informed adults do not is that there is something radically unique about my son, and it is not limited to his almond-shaped eyes, his lazy tongue, and small, low-set ears. He is ready and willing to accept you, hug you, love on you, and bless you with his joy and peace.

I believe a great deal of the church has lost this ability to freely observe, and in doing so we have missed out on tremendous blessing, joy, and peace.

The skill of observation is summed up by the ability to see details that are staring us in the face but have never been pointed out before. It is the honest cataloging of all data, whether we understand why it is in the story or what purpose it serves. It means fighting the human inclination to see what we are looking for and not what is there, because, as H. M. Tomlinson beautifully put it, "We see things not as they are, but as we are."[2]

The serious observer must consider four categories when approaching any situation:

What I know

What I think I know, but don't really know

What I know I don't know

What I don't know that I don't know

Any explorer worth her salt will admit there are things in each of the above categories as she embarks on her exploration. Healthy observation is a process of humility, conflict, and adventure. Learning something new about ourselves and the world in which we live inevitably produces experiences of discomfort, confusion, insecurity, and fear. We don't like admitting there are things we don't know, or perhaps worse, things we thought we knew, but about which we were wrong. Yet observation demands this courage because Scripture is worth it. It is fascinating. People are interacting with the divine and recording their experiences, transcendence is somehow becoming imminent, and God is pursuing humanity. I can think of nothing better on which to use my skills of observation.

Winning an argument or stacking up more verses to prove oneself right does not give anyone the right to punish, ostracize, or persecute someone with a different opinion. Truth is not the sum of an equation. Truth is an atmosphere that encourages creativity, allows for mistakes, and celebrates the courage to challenge the past as we adventure into knowing God more fully.

Observation is powerful. Strengthening this skill will affect other areas of our lives as well because we can begin to better observe our choices, motives, family culture, church community atmosphere, narratives our parents tell us, and the themes handed to us from church history and orthodoxy.

Let's try it out. Without looking up the passage in Genesis 3, answer the following: When Adam and Eve ate from the tree which God instructed them not to eat of, who was cursed? What were the consequences?

Now, open your Bible and read the passage. Observe. The word *curse* is used by the author of Genesis in reference to both the *serpent* and the *ground*. There is no indication that the man or the woman is cursed. For some, their Bible narrative and gospel story included the idea that humanity was cursed. Why? It certainly isn't a part of the story the author of Genesis is telling. If you fall under that category, you may want me to explain away your prethought that humanity is cursed, instead of allowing the absence of the data that would support your conclusion to give you pause. You may have to live with some unresolved internal conflict before you decide to either reaffirm your prethought or strike out in a new direction.

Ultimately, we must decide if we will take responsibility for our own observations, opinions, and choices, or if we will abdicate this foundational attribute of our identity to another. There is a preponderance of information out there. Don't misunderstand me: I think God has used good and honest thoughts of humans to further his kingdom. There are men and women in our time and throughout history who seem to have a profound understanding of Scripture and who have made helpful, enriching, and even divinely inspired contributions to the world of commentary. There are those whose vast knowledge of language, history, and culture are an invaluable resource as we go on our journey. However, all of this wealth of information must still be treated as opinion. Educated, informed, even inspired opinion? Sure. But still opinion.[ii] I encourage you to observe the text and decide for yourselves what the authors of Scripture intended

---

[ii] To go into detail about what weight we should give these sources would require us to delve into epistemology: what vehicles we give credibility to as we gather data and form our opinions. Cognitively driven people would place higher value on doctorates, books, and logic. Intuitive souls would value experience, spiritual discernment, and events that move them emotionally. Opinions carry the weight we give them. The weight we give them differs from person to person, temperament to temperament, culture to culture, gender to gender, etc. You must decide.

to communicate to their readers. From this raw data, you will form your own conclusions. But remember, those too will only be opinions. This journey for truth is a marathon, not a sprint.

Tool #2: Unresolved

If you commit yourself to a blank canvas as you open to the first page of Genesis, and if the only agenda you bring with you into your personal adventure of exploring Scripture is observation, the next tool you will discover through your process of observation will be the presence of the unresolved. If observation drives our process forward, we will constantly be adding to our knowledge of the text. The very nature of this process will demand that we often live with unresolved ideas, unanswered questions, and loosely held opinions (as we continue to study and gather more data).

$$\frac{(\text{Observation} \times \text{Permission for the Unresolved}) + \text{Historical Information}}{} = \frac{\text{A greater chance to hear}}{\text{the author's original intent}}$$

Many years ago, when our family was comprised of a respectable number of kids (five), a little seven-year-old boy named Jerry came to live with us. He was angry. I don't mean he had a temper or that he was angry the day he got to our home, or any other kinds of *angry* that I had experienced in my sheltered Christian life. I mean anger was his culture, his constant companion.

If you can imagine the coping mechanisms developed by a helpless child to deal with a consistent and reckless flow of aggressive, violent, and terrorizing experiences day after day, year after year, you may begin to understand the root system of my son's anger.

The day he arrived, my four sons and one daughter were excited and curious to have a new little brother. My four oldest tried to connect with the new kid, including him in their games, climbing trees, jumping on our trampoline, and showing him their rooms with all their treasures. It wasn't long, however, before the limited skill sets of two thirteen-years-olds, a twelve-year-old, and an eleven-year-old were frustrated and thwarted in their attempts to connect with our new arrival.

They realized that the new kid was going to be difficult. Jerry antagonized them with his mouth. Belligerent, snide, sarcastic, and arrogant comments came out in a constant torrent until each of my beautiful, patient kids had enough.

As I observed these interactions, my heart began to break. I realized just how great the gulf was between us and this precious little guy. He had lived in a world full of angry words and actions where he never felt safe, and an internal culture that understood there was nobody he could count on to have his back. *Nobody.* It made sense, really. To him, the world was dangerous, people were mean, and anger was the only atmosphere he knew.

It came as no surprise that, as the day wore on, each of my four eldest became so frustrated with the aggression pouring out at them that they no longer wanted to play with the new kid. As they began to try to shut their doors and separate themselves from the onslaught, Jerry turned up the heat. Now, with things at a boiling point, he added punching and kicking to his repertoire, and succeeded in getting himself either punched or knocked to the ground in return.

I don't promote violence, but if you are going to have a big family, you have to get comfortable with what my family calls "the law of the jungle." In other words, kids will be kids, and I can't parent and micromanage everything, so go work it out yourselves. This *Lord of the Flies* strategy works great when you have a core of two or three kids with gentle and generous hearts at the top of the food chain. While the day had gone poorly, I was confident my older kids would rebound and try again.

Seemingly satisfied with each of his inevitable rejections from my four eldest, Jerry turned his attention to my youngest son, Bo, who happened to be only a year older than he was and who has Down Syndrome.

I was washing dishes in front of the kitchen window, which looked out into our backyard. With the window open and the curtains partly closed, I could hear Bo jumping on the trampoline, pretending to be Spider-Man. I heard the back door and then someone joining him on the trampoline. Before long I heard Bo let out a yelp and then it was quiet. When it happened again, I pulled back the curtain to get a view of the trampoline, where I saw Bo getting back to his feet, rubbing his shoulder, and Jerry jumping alongside. As I watched, Jerry jumped for few more seconds and then turned and kicked at my son's legs, knocking him down.

As I said, I'm a firm believer in the law of the jungle, but as I watched my new little assassin turn his sights on the "weak" kid, all bets were off. He punched my son again, and I wheeled to head out the door. Suddenly, though, I stopped in my tracks. *Somehow* (that's code for the Holy Spirit is real and does real stuff) I saw the reality of what was unfolding on the trampoline in my own backyard. Deep brokenness had decided to do battle with exquisite peace. For there is no other way to describe Bo: joyful, peaceful, gentle, *awesome!* He makes everyone feel included and special. So, while my protective instincts were firing on all cylinders, I felt urged to leave the situation unresolved and see what would happen. I turned back to the window and watched as that angry little boy punched, kicked, and knocked my eight-year-old down several times. Each time, the boy with the gentle almond-shaped eyes got up, grunted, rubbed the pain away, and went back to jumping, playing, and smiling. Finally, our new arrival had seen enough. He got off the trampoline and slowly walked away.

But a curious thing happened from that unresolved situation. Over the next few weeks it became evident that Bo had a new bodyguard. At the store, church, and the playground, there were now three sets of eyes constantly looking out for him. When we walked down the sidewalk, the newest member of our family would position himself between Bo and the traffic in the street. At crosswalks Jerry would take his brother's hand and keep him from going too early into traffic. When Bo contracted a severe respiratory infection and spent three days in ICU, Jerry asked incessant questions about his brother and didn't sleep well until he came home. These two unlikely brothers became known in our house as "the twins" and shared a room for most of their childhood.

As hard as it was to watch my son be hurt, and as much as I wanted to jump in and fix the situation—to bring it to a satisfactory conclusion—leaving it unresolved was powerful. It led to something even better.

It's difficult to leave things unresolved. It goes against our nature and our culture. We want to *know*—definitely. What do we fear almost more than anything else? The *unknown*. But if we are going to look at Scripture in a new way, we are going to have to become comfortable with a lack of resolution. If observation has any chance of being your primary tool for understanding Scripture, you will have to learn to live with unanswered questions, because they are everywhere in the Bible. I don't want to give you a particular example of unresolved Scripture, because what may be unresolved for me could be something to which you have come to a firm conclusion, and vice versa. It is different for us all. I may have settled in my mind what Scripture says about women in leadership, but you could still be searching for your answer.

The instruction on the use of the *unresolved* tool is simple: Let it exist. You can relax. You can hold questions at arm's length and ponder them. You won't forget them; they'll come back to you, often with more clarity over time.

As a younger man I spent some time in mathematics. It was always interesting operating with the concept of infinity. Simply put, infinity reduced even the largest finite numerical concepts to the equivalent of zero. Yet, we are beings with a finite perspective who expect resolution as we boldly proclaim that we are studying an infinite God! Insanity!

At some point we were led to believe that good theology equaled resolved theology. Those with answers are full of faith; those with questions full of doubt. We like giving statements of fact: "Those who don't pray the sinners' prayer go to hell." But this core value in the hearts of theologians that causes us to convert stories into maxims and systems is flawed, at best. Why do we distill the supple beauty and invitational mystery of prose, poetry, and parables into the hard-edged dogmas of our doctrinal statements and theological textbooks? Many theologians, Bible teachers, and book writers seem to value resolved ideas more than the unresolved. Definitive answers have become more important to us as Christ-followers than becoming like a little child so we can enter, or even see, the kingdom of heaven.

The trite yet true observation that different stories mean different things to different people not only is accurate, but has a depth of wisdom that should inform our discussion of truth. If God wants intimacy with each of us as individuals, then each of us will have unique, individual connections to the same God. Typically, this has hardly been allowed in church history, let alone celebrated. We prefer to find a group of like-minded people, with like-minded relationships with God, often leading to "house rules," the absolutes and doctrines of faith. But the demand for absolutism makes it certain that intimacy will never grow.

In the early years of my marriage I worked hard to honor the advice my father gave me to "not let the sun go down on my anger." Internally, though, I also took it to mean, "Don't let the sun go down on the unresolved." We were two separate humans with differing passions and ideas, so of course we didn't always agree. But what I discovered during those dozens, maybe hundreds, of long nights of frustration, pushing and fighting to agree, was that agreement was not necessary to intimacy. In fact, in my aggressive verbal maneuvering and waning concern for my wife's feelings, I would regularly perceive a fork in the road: press on to agreement, resolve the issue at all costs, even if we were at it until the sun came up, or . . . shut my mouth, hold her tight, and whisper, "I choose you."

There is no such thing as a resolved relationship. You can resolve mathematical equations, you can resolve law-based judgments, and you can resolve debts. What you cannot resolve is the intentional journey of two beings who have vastly different opinions, perspectives, and experiences. We can only walk together until we trust each other enough to see our situation from the other person's perspective.

The space created by the unresolved is a secret place. It is hidden from the intellect and from our dogged determination to resolve unanswered questions at any cost. It's as if God has "hidden these things from the wise and understanding and revealed them to little children" (Matt. 11:25). You see, the unresolved forces us to admit we don't know. The unresolved grows a culture of humility, exposes coercive authority, and champions the creativity of new perspectives. The unresolved demands that we find reasons other than agreement to love each other and to stay connected.

We have another important decision to consider: Is the goal of Father God's heart, the purpose of the death and resurrection of his Son, and the ministry of the Holy Spirit, to produce people who understand, know, and protect a series of beliefs, or is it to produce people who live and love like Jesus?

Tool #3: Story

As we continue to observe the text of Scripture, and as we develop the skill of not resolving questions before the text resolves our questions, we will begin to perceive that the literary medium we are interacting with in Scripture is the medium we call *story*. Story is unique as a literary medium, with a different agenda, and upon extensive observation of this medium we will begin to see how story works. Understanding that the Hebrew authors of Scripture communicated extensively through story and that even the parts of Scripture that don't appear to be story have a very specific story behind them is the third tool we will employ in our journey through Scripture.

$$\frac{(\text{Observation x Unresolved}) + \text{Historical Info}}{\text{Story}} = \begin{array}{c}\text{A greater chance to hear} \\ \text{the author's original intent}\end{array}$$

A good book is a truly magical thing. The story within its pages has the ability to transport you to faraway lands, place you in the middle of an adventure, and give a taste of attributes you don't personally possess. Well-written characters can speak to our souls, make us feel understood and less alone, and give us courage where we believed we had none. Books can help us see into places hidden from us by our socioeconomic status, geography, culture, or place in history. I loved reading to my kids and watching as the momentum of a mighty story carried them away in their imaginations or helped them understand the world in a new way.

Story is defined as: a narrative, either true or fictitious, in prose or verse, designed to interest, amuse, or instruct the hearer or reader.[3] Story is a unique method of writing, with a wide variety of classifications, or *genres*. Some of the most notable genres are fable, myth, news, and fiction, and each has its own repeated structure that, over time, teaches us how each of these genres function and how to approach the story they tell.

Take fable, for instance. One of the most famous fable writers of all time, Aesop, was consistent with the structure of his tales, which generally portrayed animals behaving like people and in need of some sort of lesson, usually mirroring vices found in the human world. As we read these stories, we expect the choices of the animals to lead to a crisis that is resolved with a moral lesson. We anticipate the sequence and are not surprised when the story ends with a positive outcome for the characters with virtuous qualities and a negative outcome for those that lack them.

Now imagine the news being written like a fable. It wouldn't work, because we expect the news to be presented in a certain way, with its own inherent structure. We would be frustrated trying to figure out who the fox represented and from what country the grapes were imported. No, though there is a great deal of blissful ignorance needed, we like to think that our chosen news source tells it to us straight. Just the facts, ma'am. Just the facts. However, while news is based on actual events, it still tells a story, as is evident by how different news outlets can make the same event appear in entirely contrasting lights.

Fable and news are great, but let's just take a moment to thank the good Lord for the genre of fiction—that glorious thing that ignited our imaginations as children and can still do so today. Fiction has characters, and as we move through the story, we are privy to their perspectives. Depending on how the author positions them, we will empathize and relate to their perspectives differently. We see the difference between first person, third person, and omniscient views, and have a general understanding, even if subconscious, of how they affect the story. Good authors know how to connect with the reader and inspire the feelings that promote the intention of their book. It's a beautiful thing.

Let us all remember to be careful with the level of authority we claim to have in our understanding of God, truth, and divine will. Atrocities have been committed and are still being tolerated in the space that over-reaching spiritual leaders have claimed to inhabit.

Scripture too is a story. Of course, it is not fable or news, nor is it fiction. So what kind of story is the Bible? Scripture moves between several diverse types of story: narrative, poetry, genealogy, apocalyptic, literature of the oppressed, and many more, and they all function differently.[4] As readers, we have been entrusted to determine what kind of story we are reading.

Humans crafted the stories in the Bible. They told us what they had observed, what the Holy Spirit showed them, what was in their hearts to pass on to others. They specifically chose which parts of their observation to include in the story and described what they observed using word pictures, themes, idioms, and other storytelling devices of their choosing. They arranged the parts of the story in ways that made sense to them, ways that were common to storytelling in their time and culture. They placed the aha moments in their stories where they determined it was appropriate, but often in a manner that we, in the twenty-first century, find unnatural, illogical, and counterintuitive. For us to understand the expected characteristics and structure of a writing, it is our duty to learn as much as we can about the culture and context of the author. To do so, we will need to do some research. But beware: There is no such thing as history written without bias. There are many wonderful authors who write about history, but they choose what to include based on their personal journeys and worldviews.[5]

Like all story, scriptural stories contain varying perspectives. It is my observation that stories that are seminal pieces of cultural history—worldview stories or metanarratives—contain three distinct perspectives that exist both separately and intermingled: human, divine, and revelation (that space in which the divine and human interact).

At one end of the spectrum we have the human perspective. In the stories of Scripture, we often meet characters who view their world through the appetites of their flesh. Without the desire or ability to perceive the world around them with their spirit, they read much of what they are experiencing from a one-sided, limited perspective that is a product of human desires, emotions, fears, and insecurities. These parts of the story are often obvious, as they are set in opposition to others who are perceiving the same event with their spirit and have a different view. Read about Elisha and his servant's inability to see the armies of the lord (2 Kings 6:15–17), or Jesus and the two on the road to Emmaus (Luke 24:13–32).

At the opposite end of the spectrum is the perspective of the divine. We envision a realm inhabited by our Creator where nothing is veiled, incomplete, or skewed by brokenness. I would argue that this perspective is flawless and whole in every way. God has no blind spots. There is no fragmenting in his perspective of his reality and his creation. We would be hard pressed to find anyone in any religion who did not see the God perspective as ultimate, accurate, and complete. It is the realm humanity seeks to understand in the face of our fragmented experience and our separation from our created identity. It is from this *divine* realm that we draw the concepts of infallibility and inerrancy and then try to import them into the *human* realm.

Many people in positions of authority, whether they be ancient prophets, kings, priests, or present-day preachers or theologians, claim to have access to this divine level of perspective. Let us all remember to be careful with the level of authority we claim to have in our understanding of God, truth, and divine will. Atrocities have been committed and are still being tolerated in the space that over-reaching spiritual leaders have claimed to inhabit.

Humans cannot help but be influenced by their humanity when trying to communicate the things of God. To put it another way, it is a serious and often dangerous claim to assert that our revelation perspective is a carbon copy of God's perspective. The realm of revelation should never be confused with God's perspective. Yes, the purpose of revelation is to expose us to God's perspective; however, humility, teachability, and room for process are necessary for negotiating the realm of revelation honestly and effectively.

Now, I am not suggesting that God cannot be known, but no one has been to heaven and returned with film footage sharing an exact revelation of God with us. Even if someone has been taken to heaven, as soon as this person uses human senses and resources to communicate what was experienced, we no longer have a perfect re-presentation of the divine, but rather a mixture of what was experienced and what that human agent perceived, interpreted, and reported using human language and concepts. This mixture—the overlapping of the divine and human perspectives—is what many cultures and religions would refer to as *revelation*, and it is the third perspective found in the Bible.

Humans cannot help but be influenced by their humanity when trying to communicate the things of God. To put it another way, it is a serious and often dangerous claim to assert that our revelation perspective is a carbon copy of God's perspective. The realm of revelation should never be confused with God's perspective. Yes, the purpose of revelation is to expose us to God's perspective; however, humility, teachability, and room for process are necessary for negotiating the realm of revelation honestly and effectively.

Scripture, like any story, moves between these three perspectives. Some parts of the story are meant to be an attempt to give us the omniscient, perfect overview of God's perspective. Others are meant to be a recording of human perspective, and some are written as an attempt to describe human interaction with God's perspective. We must have the Holy Spirit to determine which is which. We must be humble and teachable—willing to listen to others with different opinions, greater familiarity with the original languages, cultures, and values of our authors. We must see ourselves as part of communities of faith, all pursuing truth, comparing and contrasting our opinions. We must be prepared to disagree and stay connected as brothers and sisters of the same family. To play the trump card of absolutism and claim that we alone possess it is lazy and often an attempt to control the flow of truth. Absolutism is the birthplace of much persecution of those who have different opinions and ultimately an exercise not requiring the presence and leading of the Holy Spirit.

The authors of Scripture report their interactions with God from their perspective, but the church must recognize the worldview, social context, and personal makeup (temperament and experiences) inherent in that reporting. Recording revelation does not equal God's perspective. It may contain God's perspective, but is colored by human imperfection. Similarly, inspiration is not a concept that guarantees infallibility and inerrancy either. On the contrary, inspiration is a concept that describes partnership. Yes, partnership with the divine, but partnership nonetheless.

While I strongly support the notion that the words of Jesus were in fact inerrant and infallible when he spoke them, even the red-letter portions of our Gospels—where Matthew, Mark, Luke, and John relay the things that Jesus said—are recorded decades after the fact and are a product of the accuracy of the authors' memories and their storytelling agendas. Now, by faith one can assert that the Holy Spirit *inspired* these authors to remember accurately, but this would be an opinion about the text, not an assertion of the text itself.

Galatians 5:12 provides us an opportunity to see the human perspective being interjected into the divine. In Paul's letter to the Galatians church, he is frustrated with those he sees as stirring up trouble among the believers and passionately tries to protect the truth of the good news. At one point, he zealously makes the aggressive comment that he wishes those teaching the Galatians they needed to be circumcised to be justified would go the whole way and emasculate themselves. Now, close your eyes for a moment and picture the words "emasculate yourselves" on the lips of Jesus. Can you do it? Can you see the one who came to make humanity whole speaking brokenness over anyone?

Is it possible that not every piece of Paul's thoughts and character are as pure as others? Does calling the letter to the Galatians "inspired" or "God-breathed" make it perfect and without error, or has the breath of God entered the one whom God loves, producing a letter that sees the divine, yet is intertwined with humanity? Does this verse have authority? Of course it does, but not because it is perfect.

Scripture has authority because God breathed out through human authors revelation that carries the very essence of who God is. And God is confident that his partnership with Abraham and his descendants is capable of blessing all families and all nations!

> He has designed us to need and learn from each other. He will use events and experiences recorded by people who encountered him to teach us his ways, provoke conviction, correct our destructive behaviors, and train those he loves in righteousness so that all who come into Christ might be complete, equipped for the assignments God gives us. (2 Tim. 3:16–17, Dan's translation)

It can be a little scary acknowledging the overlap of these three perspectives and the effect it has on what we desire to be a consistent, universal truth. How do we decide what to take away from Scripture? How do we apply it to our lives? How does it influence us? What is God saying through Scripture, and what is our responsibility to obey it?

First, I think it is important to consider what you know of God. Contemplate your experiences with him and what he has revealed to you through his Holy Spirit about your relationship and his character. Now consider Jesus and the level of authority you give his life and teachings in your own life. Jesus said, "If you have seen me, you have seen the Father" (John 14:9 CEV), and in Hebrews 1:3 Christ is portrayed as an exact representation of the Father. Consistently in the Gospels we see Jesus using the power of storytelling to discern which hearers had the heart posture to perceive the truth of God's kingdom and which had closed their eyes and made themselves deaf to its truth. Many, it turns out, had done the latter. When Jesus encounters so many of his countrymen who cannot see the kingdom of heaven from where they stand, he challenges them to honestly assess themselves and change their position.

The overarching theme of the teachings of Jesus as recorded in the Gospels unveils a kingdom that operates differently than the polarizing values of our accepted method of pursuing truth. Jesus regularly, both in word and deed, displayed a flat refusal to be bound by the "us or them" construct with which humanity is so comfortable. He dined with the powerful and the weak, the righteous and the sinner, the insiders and the outsiders. He stopped for the outcast, the leper, the unclean woman, the pagan oppressor, the despised Samaritan, and many others who played for the other team. His conversation and conduct were not to aggressively take field position, seeking to defeat his opponents. Rather, he positioned himself relationally, *in the other team's end zone*.

The woman caught in adultery in John 8 is a fantastic example of how Jesus positioned himself on the playing field he inherited. Jesus was identified as a rabbi and functioned as a prophet. Both identities were commonplace and understood by everyone in first-century Israel. The rabbi was expected to teach and uphold the law, and the prophet was expected to call the people of God back to monogamous fidelity with their God. A woman caught breaking the law—trampling on a marriage covenant—was brought to Jesus so the leaders could have a real-time examination of Jesus's operating system. Was he a true rabbi? Was he a true prophet? Would he uphold the law? Much is made of Jesus writing in the dirt and inviting the accusers, "Let him who is without sin among you be the first to throw a stone at her" (John 8:7). What I find significant is that Jesus positioned himself down in the dirt with the accused (and *guilty!*) woman, surrounded by a ring of powerful men, presumably already holding stones, ready to do what their God "required" of them.

The accepted playing field had self-indulgent law breaking as one end zone and righteousness (defined as God-disciplined law observance) as the other. Which team was Jesus playing for? Which end zone would he defend? His answer, though silent, was a powerful roar of protest against the construct in which he was forced to operate.

His posture said, "I sit with the accused. I sit with the guilty. Go ahead, throw the stones; carry out the judgment."

> *Truth, then, is our participation in the story of Jesus. Story is not simply the container that the Scriptures come in, it is part of the revelation itself.*

Since we aren't taught to read Scripture as story, we aren't taught to see ourselves in the story with Jesus, so the tension between believing an idea about him and making a choice to act like him is missed. Others may start to throw the stones! *Breathe . . .* Jesus is in the line of fire. He will receive the same treatment as the guilty. Yes, this is his story! Where Jesus places himself in the story speaks more powerfully than the dialogue itself. It says, "You are a woman, considered less worthy than men; you are guilty of a capital crime; powerful men want to kill you; I sit *with* you, awaiting the same fate as you." That is powerful!

This is the backbone of the value system Jesus revealed. Power is not expressed in being right, sinless, or executing God's perceived will. Heaven's power is the power to sit with the "other," the "outsider," and reveal to them not only the idea or theology of redemption and salvation, but the posture—the actual behavior—that illuminates the love God has for every atom of his creation.

Not all Scripture is the same kind of truth or the same intent. Moses, David, and Nahum may have been the high-water mark of their generation, but they had never met Jesus. They had never truly seen the Father or heard his voice with the clarity that came through the Word-become-flesh. Why would we listen to Moses's council to stone the lawbreaker, or David's prayer for God to torture and kill his enemies, or Nahum's assertion that God throws filth on Nineveh, when we have seen Jesus? Jesus is our best chance to perceive God's perspective from inside the human perspective. He is our compass. He is the mountaintop. He is the perspective of heaven. He loves, feeds, heals, and generously and courageously includes the outsider. All else is inferior revelation.

Jesus *is* the story, and he too saw the power of using story. His common refrain was, "The kingdom of heaven is like . . ." The disciples were often frustrated by his use of story, and they aren't alone. It would have been so much simpler if he had just given us the truth, point by point, so that we would not get it wrong. Right? Why speak to us in parables? I believe it is because truth cannot be completely contained in an idea, maxim, or a formula. These can point us toward truth, but they are too finite, too rigid, too easily manipulated for our personal needs. No, I suspect truth is summed up in the person of Jesus—his values, how those values manifested in his choices, and his ability to do the very same things that God, his father, was doing. We grow in truth as we live as he lived. Truth, then, is our participation in the story of Jesus.

Story is not simply the container that the Scriptures come in, it is part of the revelation itself. Communicating something through the medium of story has a profoundly different outcome than giving a list, for example. The structure of the story inherently affects what we take from it. One reason I believe the structure created by story is so important to the Bible is because *truth behaves differently when contained in a story* as opposed to how it works when expressed in a formula or maxim.

Unlike a maxim, and just like Jesus did with the adulterous woman, story demands that we position ourselves *inside* the narrative to determine our perspective and consequent actions. The lessons within the words are allowed to settle slowly, in layers, seeping through the openings of our hearts like mist permeating a forest on a cool evening. We are given the chance to ponder the meaning for ourselves, and we all know we appreciate more fully that which has cost us something. Story weaves together facts, metaphors, hyperbole, word pictures, and many other mechanisms into one seamless expression.

We see this in the parable of the Good Samaritan in Luke 10. Jesus takes a simple story and blows up centuries of theology, both backward into Judaism and forward into Christianity. The victim could have been anyone. In fact, many of the listeners in the crowd that day would have positioned themselves as the victim. After all, first-century kings, let alone common people, would find our modern level of comfort, freedom, safety, and self-determination unthinkable.

The next two characters in the story were specific kinds of people: those who held political and religious authority in the world. The actions of these two characters called into question the truth of their relationship to the victim. The fourth character introduced into the story was an outsider, one who was overlooked and even despised by all who were listening in the crowd. Victims and rulers alike would have seen this Samaritan as "other" than themselves: lesser, unimportant, part of the problem and not the solution. But in this story the outsider, the rejected person, is the hero. He stops. He cares. He heals. He pays. He serves. He sacrifices.

Where do you see yourself in the story? Who was the *true* neighbor? This is how Jesus invites his followers to live. If we insisted on boiling this story down to a maxim or formula, we *could* say things like: Only outsiders can be true neighbors; or, no religious or political leader or person of influence can be a true neighbor. But requiring a maxim from such a story can clearly lead us to obvious error.

One of the beauties of story is that it is imprecise. It does not establish systems of thinking or construct formulas for evaluating others. Story requires that we look at truth from different perspectives. It keeps one person, or one group of people, from being able to claim a corner on the truth market. Do you know how hard it is for most Americans to perceive the perspective of a victim—the perspective that so much of scriptural story speaks from and to? We love so autonomously, powerfully, freely, comfortably, and securely. There is a truth to the perspective of the victim, the impoverished, the oppressed that is largely ungraspable by the wealthy, the strong, and the protected. In the context of first-century Israel, the summation of the Good Samaritan story is that Jesus teaches that right living (righteousness) is determined by real-time choices made in the next interaction with one's fellow man, regardless of one's perceived station in life; that righteousness is not a birthright or a possession, but rather an action of the heart.

Another layer of the Good Samaritan story is that the priests and Levites were not caring for the common man. Jesus expertly and intricately addresses both the hypocrisy of self-serving elites and the national identity of elitism with which Israel looked down their noses at the Samaritans and outsiders.

Not only does story allow truth to contain layers that a maxim does not, but it provides space for truth to unfold, and in that space, placement matters. *Truth looks different depending on where and when you are standing in the story.*

In *The Lion, The Witch, and The Wardrobe*, C. S. Lewis creates the world of Narnia and tells the metaphorical story of Aslan, the son of the emperor over the sea, who comes to Narnia to establish, protect, and redeem his people—the talking animals. At a crucial point in the story, Aslan intercedes for a traitor and relinquishes himself to the mercy of the evil, destructive element in Narnia. Lewis's powerful storytelling allows us to feel the pain, helplessness, hopelessness, and finality of the slaying of Aslan. He is bound, shaved, spit on, abused, mocked, and killed. At this point of the story, our heroines, Lucy and Susan, are living in a moment in time when reality is painful. Their experience at that juncture of the story is significant and despair seems permanent.

But the story isn't finished.

Aslan rises from the dead!

The truth of Aslan's cruel death cannot be disputed. He did in fact die, and the pain and desperation felt by those he loved was real. But were we to isolate this truth and put our focus on it outside of the context of the *rest of the story*, we would miss the far more important truth that follows: He didn't stay dead! This overarching truth, and what it meant for the Narnians, changes the entire story.

This too is how our Bible functions. The statements and assertions made, observations recorded, and truths believed at a specific point in the story cannot be understood accurately outside of the entirety of the story. What is true one day can change with the dawning of a new day. Characters in the story can actually change from heroes to villains (see Adam, Noah, Saul, David, Jonah, Peter, and Judas) and sometimes back again. Truth (theological assertions) can be added to, altered, and even exposed as false as the story continues.

Stories, in their very natures, are whole pieces of expression. The parts are always misinterpreted outside of the whole. Ignoring the universal context of story as the framework of the Bible, and pulling a verse, or several seemingly related verses, into a formula that exists outside of the story is the way we have become accustomed to hearing the great truths of our faith communicated. Much that we fight to protect as Christians is not even the story of our faith.

There is a grand narrative contained in Scripture of God's heart to create a being in his image to be a powerful force, standing face-to-face with God. The beauty, intimacy, and power of this relationship is destined by God's own will to fill the earth, to permeate the entire creation. But at different points in the story this *inevitable* plot line is in jeopardy. The characters and the "truths" espoused at these crisis points are not the destination of the story, but rather placeholders for what will come next.

Nowhere is this more evident than in the part of the story where the one who has come to redeem and recreate humanity into our rightful state is rejected, tortured, and killed on a cross. We love the cross. We put them on our churches, our houses, around our necks, and even tattoo them on our bodies. Our inability to respect the medium of story, our ignorance of Jewish thought processes, and our propensity to make story into axiomatic truth has caused two millennia of church history to focus on the wrong part of the story, and it's from this misdirection that our theologies, sermons, books, understanding of the gospel, and our treatment of one another as members of the same body all flow.

"For the joy that was set before him [he] endured the cross, despising the shame" (Heb. 12:2).

Why, oh, why do we celebrate the cross and embrace its shame? Keep reading! The story continues!

Many Jewish revolutionaries wound up on Roman crosses, but only one returned from the grave. Christ-following is not built solely and ultimately on the cross of Christ; Christ-following is built ultimately on the *resurrection* of Christ. Never have I seen an empty tomb painted on the wall of a church, or a piece of tomb jewelry that celebrates the power of our faith. Why have we paused so dramatically at a point in the story where all hope is lost instead of enduring and despising this tragic moment and leaping into the joy that was to follow?

It's because we do not understand story. We have distilled the Old Testament down to one thought: Humanity needs an atoning sacrifice, and that is answered by the cross. We have misunderstood the question and have settled on the wrong answer. We have ignored the themes of the story and have decided on a theme that fits our worldview and personal needs.

Some of us have been taught that the story begins with us and that God's behavior, his choices, are predicated on our actions. Perhaps some have even been convinced, without giving it a second thought, that their conduct is capable of blocking God's love, and thus God's love is not the most powerful force in all of creation. After all, sin and death can stop it—right?

No! The story of Scripture shows us that the love of God is immeasurably greater than we could possibly comprehend. We must return to the power of story if we are to truly understand the most important story ever written—the greatest story ever told that sometimes never really gets told.

Tool #4: Repetition

As we immerse ourselves in our observation of story and do our best to imagine a world with a mere fraction of the man-made visual content that we are bombarded with (imagine a world with very few written documents and written stories, no TV screens, movies, pictures, newspapers, magazines, billboards, advertisements, a world where the majority of people are illiterate), we will begin to see the powerful presence of certain storytelling devices that are designed to be the major indicators of what the author is trying to communicate. In a world where even written story is often experienced by the majority as listeners, hearers of the story, *repetition* comes to the forefront as the major device used by authors to communicate important themes. Thematic repetition is the fourth tool we learn to use as we travel together on our adventure with the text of Scripture.

$$\frac{(\text{Observation x Unresolved}) + \text{Historical Info}}{\text{Story} + \text{Repetition}} = \begin{array}{c} \text{A greater chance to hear} \\ \text{the author's original intent} \end{array}$$

Chapter 5

Watching my children grow and learn new things is one of the tremendous joys of fatherhood. Those who have children (or been around them for any length of time) can marvel with me at the many seeming miracles that take tiny, helpless babies and transform them over time to people who can walk, read, write, and do things like advanced mathematics. One thing that becomes clear early on is that children learn by repetition. How many times did you read that book or sing that song, or touch your chest and say "Daddy" or "Mama"? Before our children could read, we read to them, and they often wanted to hear the same stories over and over. Indeed, if we wanted them to learn a particular story, it was necessary for us to do so.

As adults we function in much the same way. While the invention of the smart phone has changed the way we learn and communicate, if there is a piece of information we want to know without resorting to a book or tech device, we have to repeat it.

Repetition was key in the ancient world, where most were illiterate. That time was (blissfully?) void of the cacophony of visual and auditory stimuli that we experience today. A world without a printing press. A world without books. A world without televisions, computers, smart phones, tablets, and radios. In that particular time of cultural evolution, story reigned supreme. When the stories of Genesis were created and eventually written, storytelling was one of the few mediums available for communicating extensive communal, spiritual, and historical information. The devices used in that storytelling become crucial for the hearer or reader to observe in order to understand the meaning of the storyteller.

There were no illustrated copies of the Hebrew Scriptures. There were no capital letters or bold fonts, no italics or multicolored ink. Storytelling developed and used specific devices to put forth themes and to hold the reader's attention. Repetition was one such storytelling device. Recurring words, phrases, and word pictures are crucial to follow if we are to understand the direction and intention of our biblical stories.

Some of these themes are traceable through individual books of the Bible. Some are so pervasive in Hebrew culture that we find different authors picking up threads of the same theme and developing them further.

Repetition was how people learned and passed significant information down through the generations. Repetition formed their identities. It wasn't done willy-nilly, but rather the importance of repetition meant that the choice of words and their delivery was calculated and intentional.

For instance, in Genesis 1 we have a written representation of what many scholars believe to be an oral tradition. The systematic repetition of "And God said," "Let there be," "It was good," and "There was evening and morning" are examples of repetition that most likely have their basis in a structure that aids in memorization and consistent transference of the story from one generation to another. While what follows is my opinion, I offer it as an example of allowing the text to guide me to my questions and ultimately to my hypothesis as to what Scripture is communicating.

Starting in verse 11, as God begins to create the living parts of his creation, he declares that they shall reproduce "according to their own kind," a phrase that will recur ten times in the next fourteen verses. At the pinnacle of this explosion of biology, God declares that he intends to "make humankind in our image, after our likeness. . . . God made humanity in his own image" (Gen. 1:26–27 NET).

If I practice the tool of observation, it is possible that I will collect data that causes disconcerting questions to present themselves to me. If I allow myself to leave them unresolved and then observe over time how these unresolved questions begin to grow and shift my understanding of the story, it occurs to me that a rather monumental idea may lie at the end of this oft repeated phrase in Genesis 1.

Is God creating humanity after his own kind?

What is suggested or implied by the image and likeness we bear?

How much like God are we?

The author of Genesis takes this repeated phrase of "own kind" from Genesis 1 and culminates the story of creation with the idea of humanity being created in the likeness of God. While we will discuss in a later chapter the significance of God naming his creation in Genesis 5:2, it is important to note that the naming statement in verse 2 is sandwiched between a reiteration of humanity being created in the likeness of God in verse 1 and another naming statement in verse 3: "When [humanity] had lived 130 years, he fathered a son in *his own likeness*, *after his image*" and named him Seth (emphasis added).

If we can set aside for a moment our theology concerning the fall of humanity in chapter 3, we will see that despite whatever shifted or changed in that moment, our author is asserting that the "likeness" of God is still intact. Furthermore, this likeness is being passed on to one he has created, who in turn is procreating in his own "likeness" and "image."

Is it possible that we are more like God than we have been led to believe?

Read the Bible with an eye toward repeated words, phrases, and themes. Listen to whole books of the Bible, and see what your mind hears when your eyes are not engaged. Take note of these repetitions, and let your heart and mind ponder their meaning through seasons of growth and Scripture study. Let the Holy Spirit lead you to see meaning in the repetition.

Tool #5: Intent

As we observe the text of Scripture again and again, allowing our informed opinions to evolve without resolving questions that remain unresolved in the text, as we observe how story functions and how important to biblical authors the device of thematic repetition is, we will begin to ask very unsettling questions: "What is the *intent* of Scripture? What do the authors of Scripture think they are doing? What perspective are they writing from, and how accurate is that perspective?" Put another way: "Does all of the text of our Bibles have the same intent?"

$$\frac{(\text{Observation x Unresolved}) + \text{Historical Info}}{\text{Story} + \text{Repetition}} = \frac{\text{A greater chance to hear}}{\text{the author's original intent}}$$

Repetition is important, and it needs to be connected to our goal of perceiving the author's intended meaning. A repeated theme in our home was that of belonging. With children joining our family in so many different stages from such varying backgrounds, it was important that they knew they had a place with us. Everything my wife and I did was intended to show them these simple yet profound truths: They were loved. They were wanted. They belonged.

Sometimes it was difficult to make them see the reality of these truths. Such was the case for our first daughter. She joined our family at the age of eleven, after having been passed, along with her three younger siblings, from one foster family to another. Her previous foster family had adopted her three younger siblings, but couldn't go through with adopting her, because the behavior brought on by years of neglect and pain were just too much for them to handle.

When Family Services explained the situation and asked if we would take her, we knew it would be a long road, and what followed was indeed a long period of frustration and hope. Through sheer will and the supernatural love and patience available to us through the Spirit of Christ, we gave our first daughter everything we had: attention, hugs, gifts, love, patience, discipline, vacations, prayer, and times of intimate worship where I know she at least felt God's love. All of this was done with the intent to show her she was loved, she was wanted, she belonged. In spite of all this, we rarely saw emotion from her. She never hugged her mother or showed us affection, and while we constantly pursued her with openness and warmth, for three years we never saw past her extensive emotional defenses.

On her third Christmas with us, my wife and I wanted to get her the perfect canopy bed, and we finally found it: cast iron forest green, inlaid with vines and leaves. Once we added gauzy white linens, it looked like a bed fit for a princess. On Christmas morning, after all the presents were unwrapped, one of my kids noticed a string tied to the base of the tree, running behind the couches and down the stairs.

"What's up with the string?" my son asked.

"At the end of the string is a present for your sister," we replied.

When our tribe realized that the one girl in the family had been selected for a special Christmas present, the excitement grew, and all eyes turned to our daughter, who took off with her brothers to follow the string.

I must confess: I'm a little twisted. That string was close to half a mile long and led around our very large property, finally leading them to the workshop. When my daughter saw the bed, she looked at her brother with an odd expression of confusion and tightly wound excitement. She couldn't or wouldn't move or talk.

"The bed's for you," my son said.

Slowly she walked over, climbed on the bed, spread out her arms as if to hug the mattress, and started to cry. She told me later she had never had anything so nice and didn't think she deserved to have something so valuable.

One could look at this story and say that our purpose in choosing that bed was to give our daughter a place to sleep, but that would be missing the entire point. We already had beds. Our intent as parents, as the authors of this little story in our daughter's life, was for her to experience extravagant love. We knew she needed to feel permanency. Like any little girl, she needed to know she was the cherished one in her own story. We were writing a story of love and belonging for our daughter, and we used a bed. God has written a story of love and belonging for his people, and he used (and is using) Scripture to tell it.

The Bible is a compilation of shorter books that have been gathered together in one place.

We must be free from the tyranny of absolutism. No author of Scripture considered that he was writing timeless, absolute truth.

For centuries they were separate scrolls and handled exclusively by a select few. The purpose of these scrolls, the *intent* of the authors, was to tell the story of Israel's God as creator, covenant maker, and rescuer from exile.

The tool of intent is the sum and product of using the other four tools well. Many of us have been taught to approach Scripture with these questions at the forefront of our minds: "What does this text mean for me?" or "What does Scripture demand of me?" Coupled with the fact that Scripture is presented to us as inerrant, infallible, and timeless truth, the intent of the authors is locked away behind an impenetrable wall of absolutism.

Let me suggest to you that the authors of Scripture had specific ideas, audiences, and experiences in mind when they penned their text. The universality and absolutism with which we today approach their carefully tailored stories, which were intended to address specific people in specific situations, blinds and cripples us in our attempt to understand their intent. The Bible student who can ask the question, "What is the author's intent?" before asking "What does this text mean for me?" has taken a quantum leap forward in the honest assessment of these ancient texts.

It may feel daunting, but discovering the author's intent is not impossible. Many books of the Bible contain introductions and summary statements that help us discover the author's intent. In addition, reading entire books of the Bible at one sitting helps us see the contents as a whole unit, which is how the texts were meant to be seen. Many scriptural authors introduce the themes that are important to them early in their story, and our attention to these observable themes as they develop help us honestly build an understanding of the author's intent.

There is no shortcut here. If you want to know, you will have to dig. There are ample resources available to us as we seek to better understand the historical context of the authors we value so greatly. Research, archeology, and academia is always evolving and progressing as we wrestle with the limited data we have access to as twenty-first century humanity looking back at cultures hidden by the passing of time. I recommend reading historical works that look inside and outside of Christendom to report and explain the pieces of history to which we have access. Works that consider the Dead Sea Scrolls are a necessity, as this incredible find has provided data that may change some of our prethought regarding the nature of Scripture, ancient Jewish thinking, and messianic expectations.

Internally, Scripture bears witness to this time-sensitive quality of biblical revelation. In many places, Scripture itself tells us to favor one text over another or to forget previous ideas and move on to new ones. Prophets urge the people of God to forget the past and move on to the new thing; Jesus tells his followers to value certain Scriptures over others; Paul reframes Old Testament Jewish ideas through the resurrection of Jesus.

Remember, this is a marathon, not a sprint. This journey to explore and discover the intent of Scripture will be a lifelong habit of those who are truly interested in allowing the intent of the authors of Scripture to shape their understanding of the Bible.

Familiarity with the languages of the Bible—Hebrew, Greek, and a little
Aramaic as well— will aid our journey of exploration. For those who feel they
either do not have the capacity for this kind of study or do not have access
to the resources necessary, let me suggest a simple aid for holding preachers
and commentary writers accountable. Read the Bible in different translations.
Read commentaries from widely different corners of Christendom. It would
be enlightening, and probably a bit offensive, for the average Protestant to read
biblical commentaries written by Greek Orthodox or Catholic authors. You
will find different word choices selected by translators if you read the English
Standard Version, New King James, Revised Standard, or New International
Version. I would advise you to mix in some paraphrases as well, such as the
Living Bible, Passion Translation, or the Message Bible, to engage the less
cognitive, more emotive part of your soul. After all, Scripture should be studied,
but it also needs to be felt and experienced.

Equally important as you engage history in your journey of exploration into
Scripture will be the need to not cripple the author's intent with the unexamined
supposition that he is looking at his text the same way, with the same values and
thought patterns, with which we are looking at the text. Does the author believe
what he is writing is absolute and inerrant? Does the author know he is writing
our Bibles? Does the author intend for our need for absolute truth to color our
assessment of his text? Does the author think his text is timeless and applicable
across time, culture, and context?

We must be free from the tyranny of absolutism. No author of Scripture
considered that he was writing timeless, absolute truth. Rather, I suspect that
individual men, who partnered with and were breathed on and in by the
Spirit of God, communicated their personal experiences and their personal
understandings so that those to whom they wrote would more effectively hear
God's voice.

Internally, Scripture bears witness to this time-sensitive quality of biblical
revelation. In many places, Scripture itself tells us to favor one text over another
or to forget previous ideas and move on to new ones. Prophets urge the people of
God to forget the past and move on to the new thing; Jesus tells his followers to
value certain Scriptures over others; Paul reframes Old Testament Jewish ideas

through the resurrection of Jesus.

Becoming familiar with the intent of scriptural authors is the product of intentional study. Reading and rereading a book, all the while observing repeated phrases and ideas, taking the time to use a lexicon to become familiar with the breadth of meaning of a particular Hebrew or Greek word, and formulating opinions as to what the intent of the author might be, will together launch us into the adventure of discovery we were all intended to navigate.

The ideas acquired from observations will live for a season as your unresolved opinion. You will speak to others, make value judgments, and by faith employ your hypothesis in your life choices. You will observe what is growing in your mind and heart. You will notice a harvest—what is the fruit of your present understanding of Paul, Peter, Moses, or David? You have the right to evaluate the harvest: Is this fruit beneficial and in line with the character of God? Take a season to rest and then plant again, changing your opinion, adding to your understanding, and growing in your faith.

> For no good tree bears bad fruit, nor again does a bad tree bear good fruit, for each tree is known by its own fruit. For figs are not gathered from thornbushes, nor are grapes picked from a bramble bush. (Luke 6:43–44)

> Dan's translation:
> Truth aligned with God's heart will inevitably grow fruit much more congruent with heaven's culture than the current common experience of lives struggling to survive, or worse. Lies, coercive, fear-based authority, and values that are not God's heart cannot produce lives that are thriving, fulfilling, and peaceful. You can tell the source of a belief system's prethought by what it produces in the lives that attend to it. The qualities of God's heart, flourishing in a human soul, do not come from any root system other than the Tree of Life.

I cannot underestimate the importance of reading and rereading the Bible, cover to cover. It is my hope that by implementing the tools of observation, living with the unresolved, acknowledging the power of story, seeing the importance of repetition, and discovering the heart of the author's intent, we will discover truths we never noticed before. Empowered by the Holy Spirit, we will go further up and further in on this journey with God than we ever thought possible.

PART 2:

TOOLS IN ACTION

Chapter 6

Journey Away from Fear:
A Study of the Gospel of Luke

I must confess, I have a somewhat serious social issue. I am an East Coast born-and-bred, Jewish personality that has plopped down in small town Montana. Sometimes I am misunderstood. No, I'm not loud, I'm passionate. I'm not opinionated, I'm well educated. I'm not rude, I'm pleasantly animated. Do you see my problem? It isn't *me*, it's them! I swear!

Well, at any rate, sometimes the conversations I have in public are (mysteriously) overheard. Such was the case one day with a friend over lunch as we discussed faith and how God pursues us with his love. Before we left the restaurant, the owner came over to me and said, "I couldn't help overhearing your conversation. Are you a pastor?"

"Yes," I replied.

Looking down at her feet, she mumbled, "I'm sorry to bother you, but can I ask you a question?"

She then proceeded to tell me a tragic story. A year earlier her two-year-old grandson was murdered. This appalling, violent event so impacted her family that one of her daughters—the child's aunt—had committed suicide, and her other daughter—the child's mother—was coping by escaping into drugs and was also suicidal.

She finished with, "My church teaches that if people kill themselves they go straight to hell. Is that true?"

Instantly I could see the text she had probably heard: "If anyone destroys God's temple, God will destroy him. For God's temple is holy, and you are that temple" (1 Cor. 3:17). I felt both sadness at the reality that this church-going

Christian woman was unable to find hope in the body of Christ, and anger that we, as Bible teachers, often regurgitate what seminary professors and commentary writers have said without investigating, weighing, and deciding for ourselves. As a result, we leave in our wake the emaciated hope of people living in real time, with real pain, caused by real tragedy.

I replied, "No, sweetheart. His love never fails. He has always loved your daughters and your grandson, and he always will. He is with us in our pain, and he holds us in our times of loss, betrayal, and weakness."

What gives me the right to speak to her about the eternal destiny of her children, ignoring the commonly held interpretation of this text? I read, reread, observed, and examined Paul's entire corpus, listening to Paul's words through the filter of Jesus as presented in the Gospels. I study continually the culture of our biblical authors to try and understand the values, national identities, prevailing worldviews, and the hope that went into the creation of their inspired text. I *don't know for certain*, but I have come to the conclusion that God's heart for humanity looks like Jesus, and that Paul's recitation later in the same letter as the above abused text describes the way God loves us:

Have you heard?

> Love is patient and kind; love does not envy or boast; it is not
> arrogant or rude. It does not insist on its own way; it is not
> irritable or resentful; it does not rejoice at wrongdoing, but
> rejoices with the truth. Love bears all things, believes all things,
> hopes all things, endures all things. Love never ends. (1 Cor.
> 13:4–8)

This woman's experience with the doctrine of hell isn't an isolated incident. Many readers will know well similar scenarios. In another instance, I was talking with a good friend who had heard a sermon on Luke 12:4–5:

> I tell you, my friends, do not fear those who kill the body,
> and after that have nothing more that they can do. But I will
> warn you whom to fear: fear him who, after he has killed, has

authority to cast into hell. Yes, I tell you, fear him!"[i]

My friend continued, "The preacher said that I should fear God because he can throw me into hell. Is that true?"

Sadly, those who trust us as pastors and teachers have been bullied by fear-filled interpretations of texts that should require extensive examination to even enable us to hold an opinion. We have insisted on doctrinal absolutes that we can't possibly know for certain and have effectively taught that God is a tyrant who uses fear as his greatest weapon.

The Christianity that most of us have always known revolves around salvation and the ultimate destiny of humanity. *Heaven or hell*? That is the flagship concept that drives much Christian doctrine, practice, and teaching. We were born into this narrative; it is likely all we've ever known. It is what many well-meaning religious workers have proclaimed in an effort to stay true to their education. For many beloved sons and daughters of the King, it would be impossible to conceive of any other controlling narrative than the one their parents, grandparents, and great-grandparents taught them. When we encounter texts like this, our prethought takes over, and we see what we are predisposed to see.

Jesus said a peculiar phrase several times as he taught and revealed the kingdom of heaven in Israel so many years ago: "He who has ears to hear let him hear" (Matt. 11:15; Mark 4:9; Luke 8:8; 14:35). This concept is a substantial theme in the Gospels. Jesus is pointing out that we hear exactly what the orientation of our hearts allows us to hear. "He who has little, what he has will be taken away. He who has much will be given even more" (Matt. 13:12; 25:29; Mark 4:25; Luke 8:18; 19:26). So unfair! Until we realize that Jesus is not happy about this, that he is simply teaching us how the orientation of the heart affects what we can receive as seekers of truth.

---

[i] All of my research agrees that original Greek texts were written with uniform case. The mere fact that many translations do not capitalize the pronouns in verse 5, some translations capitalize all of the pronouns in verse 5, and still others only capitalize the final *him* points to editorial theologies leaking into the text.

"With the measure we use it will be measured to us" (Matt. 7:2; Mark 4:24; Luke 6:38). Does one deal in fear, control, suspicion, and accusation? Is there only a small part of one's narrative that allows for generosity, extravagant kindness, and the inclusion of others? Well then, what kind of story will he or she hear when reading the Bible, listening to a sermon, or deciding what's happening in the world? If the ear is predisposed to hearing a sin story wrapped around fear, then that is likely what will be heard.

However, if we are inclined to hearing a story of grace, it is much more likely we will see the goodness of God wrapped around his love every time we pick up our Bible. When we listen to people with different perspectives and experiences, it is possible to create a place for them in our personal narrative. And despite the evil in the world, we will be more likely to see the life-giving hand of God at work all around us.

We can continue to see what we have been told to see, accepting prethought as fact, or we can take back control and decide for ourselves. In order to accomplish this, we have to practice our skill of observation, allow unresolved questions to be included in our process of Bible study, acknowledge the structure of story and the power of thematic repetition, and seek out the author's intent.

As previously discussed, when we approach a passage of Scripture with the intent to observe, we must first remove expectation and preconceptions of its meaning. Take a breath. Relax. Remember, we are explorers, not policemen. Imagine walking through a garden, the beautiful life-giving garden of the words of our beloved Jesus, of whose care and love for us there can be no doubt. See the beautiful colors. Smell the aroma of life. Let him who has ears hear the birds singing a song of joy! Go ahead, pick a flower. Feel its soft silkiness between your fingers. Taste and see that our King is good.

Now consider the passage from Luke again, as if for the first time, and see through the paradigm of what you know about Jesus:

> I tell you, my friends, do not fear those who kill the body,
> and after that have nothing more that they can do. But I will
> warn you whom to fear: fear him who, after he has killed, has
> authority to cast into hell. Yes, I tell you, fear him!

Chapter 6

The church has taught Luke 12:4–5 as a story about God's omnipotence, sovereignty, and judgment. We attempt to perceive the meaning of the story through our expectations, current theology of the afterlife, and unquestioned belief of God's practice of casting people into hell.

But you cannot stick a syringe into the Gospel of Luke, pull out a core sample, and say what these verses mean or that said meaning is "true" when separated from the story as a whole. These two verses are part of a larger story, a life-changing one, written by an educated man two thousand years ago whose storytelling devices, rules, and patterns were markedly different from ours. Luke specifically tells us that he has thoroughly researched all that has happened so that he can tell the true story of the rabbi from Nazareth—the one about whom everyone is talking—effectively to his friend, Theophilus.

Like any story, Luke's Gospel is intended to be read and heard as one complete unit. As one becomes more familiar with the story as a whole, it is easier to understand why individual parts of the story are placed where they are and why the author arranged the smaller stories the way that he did. In short, we begin to observe his intent. Once we do so, it becomes harder to sustain theologies that pull individual verses out of their context, divorcing key statements in a smaller unit of the story from the flow and intent of the narrative as a whole.

In other words, Luke 12:4–5 does not exist in a vacuum. It is not a piece of truth detached from the rest of the words Jesus spoke or the words Luke wrote before and after these verses. These two verses are connected to those that came before and will come after. In fact, what we call chapter 12 of the Gospel of Luke is also connected to the chapters that come before and the chapters that come after. *Statements in Scripture are not truth unless they are received as connected to the story in which they are found.*

Church history has all but guaranteed we make this error. To begin, in-text divisions into chapters, verses, and paragraphs, accompanied by the editors' headings, were not a part of Luke's original story. Chapter 11 was not separated from chapter 12 until the twelfth century, and the verse divisions were not added until the sixteenth century. Why is this important? Visual arrangement or structure affects how we hear and perceive the text. Separating chapter 12 from chapter 11 begins to give us permission to separate the content of chapter 12 from the content of chapter 11. Can you imagine picking up *Lord of the Rings* for the first time and simply beginning midway through the book? Of course not!

Don't get me started on the prethought behind paragraph headings that are added to many translations as "helpful" editorial compasses directing us to look for certain ideas in the coming chapter. The English Standard Version, the New King James Version, the New International Version, the New American Standard, and many others *add* paragraph headings that redirect our attention to the translators', editors', or publishers' theologies and prepare us to hear what somebody else has already decided is the intended meaning. The Holman Christian Standard Bible actually places a paragraph break between Luke 12:3 and Luke 12:4 and titles this section "Fear God."

When we look at the Gospel of Luke as segmented parts, it is easy to overlook that Luke has been telling a story for quite a while before we get to chapter 12:4–5. Much has happened, and Luke has already begun to develop themes.

In the beginning of his story, Luke records many of the prophetic expectations that angels and people have declared over this unique child. It is here that he introduces us to the themes he will be developing throughout his narrative. Remember Simeon?

> And Simeon blessed them and said to Mary his mother,
> "Behold, this child is appointed for the fall and rising of many
> in Israel, and for a sign that is opposed (and a sword will pierce
> through your own soul also), *so that thoughts from many hearts
> may be revealed*." (Luke 2:34–35, emphasis added)

And Jesus says, after telling the parable of four kinds of soil that receive seed, "For nothing is hidden that will not be made manifest, nor is anything secret that will not be known and come to light" (Luke 8:17).

Luke has developed a theme of Jesus's life and ministry as being a catalyst for revealing or uncovering what is hidden. Here in Luke 12 he develops this theme even further. This part of the story is about revealing what previously was concealed.

What has been happening in the story? In this particular portion, Jesus has just finished speaking directly to the scribes, Pharisees, and lawyers. Stern rebukes from Jesus toward these leaders of Israel culminate in the charge that Jesus lays at their feet: "For you have taken away the key of knowledge. You did not enter yourselves, and you hindered those who were entering" (Luke 11:52).

> As he went away from there, the scribes and the Pharisees began to press him hard and to provoke him to speak about many things, lying in wait for him, to catch him in something he might say. In the meantime, when so many thousands of the people had gathered together that they were trampling one another, he began to say to his disciples first, "Beware of the leaven of the Pharisees, which is hypocrisy. Nothing is covered up that will not be revealed, or hidden that will not be known. Therefore whatever you have said in the dark shall be heard in the light, and what you have whispered in private rooms shall be proclaimed on the housetops." (Luke 11:53–12:3)

His indictment is followed immediately by the author's bird's-eye view of the players in this story. The scribes and the Pharisees are pressing Jesus hard, trying to incriminate him by something he might say. This is juxtaposed with the thousands who were "trampling each other" in their fervor to see and hear Jesus. Luke is making the point that there are two groups in Israel: those who are scheming to protect the status quo, and those who are excited that something important is happening. The seasons are changing.

Jesus then continues his censure of the Pharisees as he warns the crowd, his fellow Jews, to "Beware the leaven of the Pharisees, which is hypocrisy." *Leaven* is a concept used in Scripture to refer to an influential source. As a little leaven can cause an entire batch of dough to change and rise and become bread, so too the teachings of the influential can shape the hearts of those around them to become attentive to certain values—good or bad. *Hypocrisy* is a Greek concept that means to play act, to falsely act as something you are not.

What follows next we would expect to be connected to this introductory statement regarding the hypocrisy of the Pharisees. Jesus speaks of how what the Pharisees say and do behind closed doors, that which is "hidden," will be made known to all. He then implores his people—brothers, sisters, distant cousins, friends—to "not fear those who kill the body, and after that have nothing more that they can do" (12:4).

It is important to note that among these very same Pharisees were those who sat on the Sanhedrin, that ruling body of elders who taught the Law, judged the people according to their interpretation of the Law, and enforced the Law. Most of us twenty-first century western people living in a democracy are largely ignorant of the culture of fear created by the marriage of religious law and civil authority. We have no grid for moral failure being examined by religious authority and followed by a binding judgment. As seen in the story of the woman caught in adultery, this process is nothing short of an atrocity when a capital offense is in play. And when we observe the connective tissue of that story, we realize the process resulting in the sentence of death by stoning could begin *in the temple*! How many times did worshippers witness the horror of execution at the hands of their spiritual leaders? There is ample reason to "fear those who kill the body." We must remember that Jesus was addressing the hypocrisy, and now the coercive fear used by the ruling class in Jerusalem to keep the masses in line. Who can question the controlling narrative of Israel and live to tell the tale? The answer: No one. Not even Jesus.

And now we come to the "scary" part. Jesus says, "But I will warn you whom to fear: fear him who, after he has killed, has authority to cast into hell. Yes, I tell you, fear him!" When reading those words, many will have the same confused and fearful questions: Who is Jesus speaking about? Whom should we fear? Who kills? And after he kills, who casts people into hell?

I would propose to you that the lack of observation, coupled with absence of historical information, has led to flawed conclusions.[ii] Please note that my opinion is below, based on the data I have collected. Remember, I am not selling a better theology (although I preach one). I am giving you permission to live outside of absolutism, fear, and the tyranny of orthodoxy. I would be pleased if my thoughts on the subject gave you pause and caused you to dig and struggle in order to come to your own conclusions.

Many are aware that the Greek word translated *hell* in our English Bibles is the Hebrew word Gehenna or Ge–Hinnon. This is the place name for the Valley of Hinnon, a valley just outside of Jerusalem that had a well-known and tragic history. It is here, in this low place, that ancient kings of Israel worshipped Molech, the god of the underworld, by sacrificing their own children in fire. It was this Valley that Israel believed was cursed and consequently had become a dumping place for carcasses, entrails, and ashes. A body thrown onto this ever-smoldering trash heap was clearly cursed. And once the body and bones were burnt to ash, that person's hope in the resurrection of the righteous, the divine reconstruction of new flesh and blood around their dried bones, was all but gone.

Though we may not always be aware of or acknowledge it, first-century Israel had an eschatology. They had a hope. Their Scriptures led them to believe that God had promised a last days, a coming of the King, a day when God would restore all things and save them from their enemies. Prophets were key figures in this eschatology, promised to Israel in the Hebrew Scriptures. Prophets are seers. They can see into the future and report their findings to their contemporaries. *They reveal that which has been hidden.*

When observing the connective tissue and themes of the Gospels, it becomes apparent that Jesus is a prophet. He can see what is coming in the future, and, like any of a number of prophets in the story of Israel, he reports what he sees and warns God's people to make the necessary adjustments. Rome is coming. It will be horrible. "Please," Jesus begs, "don't stay under the authority of these hypocrites. Come, follow me into the kingdom of heaven. I want to save you from the coming horror that these hypocrites will bring upon themselves."

Jesus loves Israel. The heart of the Father is to call his people back to intimacy with him. God sent John the Baptist, and now Jesus, as prophets to call Israel to repentance—to leave wrong thinking behind and to return to God's

---

ii Yes, observation and historical information can still lead to flawed conclusions, but we are living through a growing season: sowing and nurturing a seed, reaping a harvest, resting, and then sowing again. These tools, this process, is a different paradigm for journeying into truth, assuming that today's opinion will be replaced with next year's growth.

way of thinking. To leave the thought processes, values, and culture created by the scribes, Pharisees, and lawyers and to come follow Jesus. Jesus can see AD 67. He knows what is coming. "How often would I have gathered your children together as a hen gathers her brood under her wings, and you were not willing!" (Luke 13:34).

He longs to protect Israel, Jerusalem specifically, and gather them under the protection of his wing. He has seen the destruction of Jerusalem. He has seen the tragic end of temple worship as it presently exists, and he has seen the suffering and horror of the last days of the city of Jerusalem. It was a truly terrible moment in Israel's history. The historian Josephus estimates that between 600,000 and 1.2 million bodies were thrown into the Valley of Hinnon/Gehenna during the Roman siege of Jerusalem in AD 67–69. Jewish beliefs in the hope of the resurrection for the righteous demanded certain burial techniques. Not only would the suffering in Jerusalem during the Roman siege be horrific, the destiny of their dead bodies would be contrary to their hope in the resurrection. No wonder Jesus is warning his countrymen!

Considering the above, let's recap:

Jesus has been speaking to the hypocrisy of the Pharisees.

The Pharisees, as part of the ruling body of the seventy-one elders of the Sanhedrin, have the authority to sentence certain lawbreakers to death.

The people who heard this teaching from Jesus heard it in Hebrew or Aramaic, and they would have heard the place name for *Gehenna* (an existing place in the near vicinity of where they were standing), not our contemporary idea of the English word *hell*.

Jesus specifically speaks about someone who *kills*.

So, in light of all this, Jesus is obviously speaking about his Father when he says to the people that they should be afraid. Right?

How? Why? Where is God mentioned in this passage? *Where do our minds go to drag God into this point of the story?* What information, experience, or memory did we access to reach the conclusion that God casts people into hell? Why do we think Jesus is teaching us to fear God?

To come to the conclusion that Jesus is talking about God here, one has to be predisposed to a story that is based on the fear that the God of the universe throws people into hell. God is not actually in these verses. One must imagine him there.

Contemplate the verses that immediately follow the text in question: "Are not five sparrows sold for two pennies? And not one of them is forgotten before God. Why, even the hairs of your head are all numbered. Fear not; you are of more value than many sparrows" (Luke 12:6–7).

Jesus moves from the monstrous behavior of Israel's ruling elite, to his prophetic foresight, which allows him to warn of a horror even greater than the religious fanaticism that bludgeons the weak and disempowered to death with stones. He then compares this abomination, this coming genocide, to the care his Father has for sparrows. It is this comparison that is meant to draw our attention. It is in this ludicrous gap between the tyranny, murder, and genocide by powerful men and the care, attention, and safety of God's love that we can see the revelation in Jesus's words. He is saying, "Fear not, you are of incredible value to God!"

Observing the thematic repetition and the flow of the narrative leading up to specific points in the story is crucial to our honest attempts to hear the author's intent. Knowing what follows a specific portion of text is equally informative and helpful for revelation.

After the often misunderstood verses of Luke 12:4–5, Luke goes on to discuss:

- How the leaders of Israel are denying who Jesus is before men and how this will play out when they come face-to-face with their God (12:8–9).
- How an even greater level of obstinate and rebellious behavior—refusing to recognize the Spirit of God—will land these leaders in even greater peril (12:10).
- How these same disciples will be accosted by these very leaders and brought into a place of accusation where they will need to defend themselves (12:11–12).
- How, like the rich fool in the parable, these leaders care for themselves and grow richer, fatter, and more comfortable in their wealth, but have not made the effort to be rich toward God by taking care of the needy around them with their wealth (12:13–21).

- How his followers should turn their attention to things of greater value than food and clothes (the passion of the ruling class, the things the powerful of this world value) and not be like the "nations of this world" (12:22–31).

On and on Luke goes, comparing the values of Jesus to the values of the scribes and Pharisees. Follow this theme, and observe the story Luke is telling: Don't fear these hypocrites who might kill you and be done with you. What should you be afraid of? Be afraid of what will happen if you do not judge rightly between the culture these men have created and the culture of God's kingdom that Jesus is putting on display for you. If you stick with these men, you will find yourself holed up in Jerusalem, under siege by the Romans, starving to death, experiencing the greatest suffering Israel has ever known, all because you missed the signs that a new season was dawning in Israel.

> He also said to the crowds, "When you see a cloud rising in the west, you say at once, 'A shower is coming.' And so it happens. And when you see the south wind blowing, you say, 'There will be scorching heat,' and it happens. You hypocrites! You know how to interpret the appearance of earth and sky, but why do you not know how to interpret the present time? And why do you not judge for yourselves what is right?" (12:54–57)

> Dan's translation:
> Jesus said to Israel, "You have great skill in interpreting the signs that prepare you for what weather is coming so you can take the appropriate action. Stop acting like you can't see what is taking place right now in Israel! You are responsible to look at what is happening and to judge for yourself what the truth is. Your lives depend on it."

The theme of Jesus as prophet is not the only one Luke carries through the entirety of his Gospel. He deals at length with the subject of fear before Luke 12:4–5 as well as after. Observing this repetition can further help us understand the author's intended meaning of Luke 12:4–5, which revolves around Jesus's statement, "I will warn you whom to fear." What has the author, the one who crafted this good news story with intent, been doing with the theme of fear?

- "Do not be afraid, Zechariah" (1:13)
- "Do not be afraid, Mary" (1:30)
- "His mercy is for those who fear him" (1:50)
- "Fear came on all their neighbors" (1:65)
- "We . . . might serve him without fear" (1:74)
- "They were filled with great fear. And the angel said to them, 'Fear not'" (2:9–10)
- "Filled with awe" (same Greek word translated *fear* in other places) (5:26)
- "Fear seized them all" (7:16)
- "And they were afraid, and they marveled" (8:25)
- "They were seized with great fear" (8:37)
- "She came trembling" (8:47)
- "Do not fear . . . believe" (8:50)
- "They were afraid as they entered the cloud" (9:34)
- "I tell you, my friends, do not fear those who kill the body, and after that have nothing more that they can do. But I will warn you whom to fear: fear him who, after he has killed, has authority to cast into hell. Yes, I tell you, fear him!" (12:4–5)
- "Fear not; you are of more value than many sparrows" (12:7)

Here are most, if not all, of Luke's intentional references to fear leading up to Luke 12. This is a theme, and it is repeated for a purpose. It has an effect on the story, especially in a world where this story would be read as a whole unit and, more often than not, heard as someone else read it.

Four times in the story before the aha moment of Luke 12:4–5, Luke records someone sent from God (angels or Jesus) saying, "Fear not" or "Do not be afraid." Eight times in Luke's story he reports that fear came on people. Each time it was in response to something God had authored in some way.

In summation: Those sent from God tell Israel to "fear not," but the people of Israel live in a culture where the life-giving goodness of God is so foreign to them that every time God authors a divine encounter, his sons and daughters respond with fear. The Greek word for *fear* carries the ideas of our English word *fear* as well as our English concept of *awe*. Theologians can debate the nuances of Greek all they want, but the story is clear: Israel does not know their God, his heart for them, or what is normal when their God shows his affection. The angels and Jesus, sent from God to reveal what God is like, instruct the people of Israel not to fear God.

Our focus point of the story repeats this major theme five times in one short quotation from Jesus:

> I tell you, my friends, do not fear those who kill the body, and after that have nothing more that they can do. But I will warn you whom to fear: fear him who, after he has killed, has authority to cast into hell. Yes, I tell you, fear him! Are not five sparrows sold for two pennies? And not one of them is forgotten before God. Why, even the hairs of your head are all numbered. Fear not; you are of more value than many sparrows." (Luke 12:4–7)

Dan's translation:
My friends, your fear is misplaced. Those who rule over you, inflicting their judgments upon you from the Law of Moses, can't really hurt you. But I have seen our nation's future. Rome is coming. Follow me into your true identity as beloved sons and daughters. Place your faith in God's goodness, not the leaven of your leaders. If you do not have ears to hear me or eyes to see when God is loving on you, you will find yourself barricaded in this very city, starving to death, awaiting the savagery of Roman killers. And when they come, not only will they kill you, they will throw your bodies in that accursed valley, Gehenna. Trust God, not these hypocrites. God cares for the least significant parts of his creation. Don't you think he will take care of you? Trust God. Follow me. Don't be afraid.

Luke continues to develop the theme of fear even after this point:

- "Fear not, little flock, for it is your Father's good pleasure to give you the kingdom" (12:32)
- "In a certain city there was a judge who neither feared God nor respected man" (18:2)
- "Though I neither fear God nor respect man" (18:4)
- "They feared the people" (20:19)
- "People fainting with fear and with foreboding of what is coming on the world" (21:26)
- "They feared the people" (22:2)

When Jesus represents the leaders of Israel in a story, or Luke speaks directly about the leaders of Israel, the leaders *always* have their attention, concern, and decision-making mechanism tuned to the wrong frequency. When Jesus speaks about who his Father is or what the kingdom of heaven is like, he *always* tells his followers, "Fear not."

And finally:

> One of the criminals who were hanged railed at him, saying,
> "Are you not the Christ? Save yourself and us!" But the other
> rebuked him, saying, "Do you not fear God, since you are
> under the same sentence of condemnation?" (Luke 23:39–40)

Is it possible that here, at the culmination of the story, at the moment when Jesus conquers the human fear of death and is about to loose resurrection reality back into God's good creation, that Luke records this statement by a condemned thief in order to contrast Jesus's lack of fear (of God or man) with the present reality in Israel: We have been taught to fear God; we have been taught that God judges us according to the Law of Moses; we have been taught that God says we will receive the punishment we deserve. But Jesus says, "Today you will be with me in paradise" (23:43). You can almost hear Jesus saying again, "Fear not."

This is all the same story. Luke is telling us that Jesus, who represents and lives out the values and culture of his father, is in constant opposition and conflict with those who have crafted a culture of wealth and convenience for themselves as shepherds when they were supposed to be caring for the sheep. This is not a story about who goes to heaven and who goes to hell. Can you see it?[iii] Somewhere between the mouth of Jesus and the pulpits under which we sit each week something has shifted. There is an enormous chasm. We are unaware of the evolution of our doctrine. We are unaware of who made which choices that brought us from a teaching designed to promote an atmosphere of care and safety to a culture of fear and a doctrine based on the belief that God kills, and when he is finished with his killing, he throws people into a medieval lake of fire to torment the unrighteous for eternity. We must ignore dozens of themes and a story that revolves around the good news that Jesus wants us to "fear not" if we are to cram the doctrine of hell into this passage. Maybe we can find our orthodox doctrine of hell elsewhere in the Bible, but certainly not here.

In Luke's story our hero tells us to "fear not" because his Father values us greatly as individuals. In Luke's story our hero longs to protect Israel from the coming destruction. In Luke's story there is much conflict between our hero and the religious authorities of his day. In Luke's story, God desires to save Israel.

My overall opinion is that Scripture does not support our contemporary doctrine of hell and eternal conscious torment for unbelieving humanity, but it bears saying again: This is not a book about hell. I honestly don't know what happens to the wicked when they die. For that matter, I don't even know who is wicked. And here is the beautiful thing: *I don't have to.* These are not questions to which I need absolute answers in order to live out my calling to draw people into his kingdom. I can live in the unresolved when it comes to the idea of hell or the afterlife, because if I wholeheartedly follow Christ, it honestly will not change how I live in the present.

[iii] This book is being presented as a travelling companion. As I have stated throughout, it is not my desire to convince anyone to agree with my theology, only to see how I have come to certain opinions through the data of Scripture. You do not need to accept that Rome is whom Jesus is talking about. If I can inspire you to dig for yourself, I have accomplished my purpose in this book. It's this effort and journey that will change the church, not agreement with another author or authority figure.

However, because the lake of fire mentioned in Revelation is an idea so often associated with the above verses of Luke 12:4–5, as well as the concept of hell in general, I feel it might be helpful for me to discuss my opinion here, in order to shed some light on any confusion readers might be experiencing.

I have already emphasized the importance of reading the Bible in its entirety, cover to cover. I have done so a great deal of times, and have, in the process, noted every reference to *fire* as it relates to God. I believe *fire* is the most common word picture used to express the presence of God in the divine story of our faith. From the burning bush, to the pillar of fire that led Israel in the wilderness, to prophetic revelations and pronouncements tying God's activities to concepts like consuming fire, burning up chaff, stubble and other combustible items, and the appearance of tongues of fire at Pentecost, there is an incredible story line of God's presence that is expressed with the different tools available to a good narrative.

I find the thematic repetition of *fire* in the Bible necessary to understand the heavily prophetic language filled with word pictures and metaphor in the book of Revelation. Is there an actual lake of fire, or is this another word picture used to express the nature of God's presence? Conventional Christian theology would tell us there is a literal lake of fire where demons are cast and tormented day and night forever. Conventional Christian theology, based largely on the book of Revelation, would tell us that this is where all those whose names were not found in the Book of Life will be thrown to suffer eternal conscious torment.

> And when the thousand years are ended, Satan will be released
> from his prison and will come out to deceive the nations
> that are at the four corners of the earth, Gog and Magog, to
> gather them for battle; their number is like the sand of the sea.
> And they marched up over the broad plain of the earth and
> surrounded the camp of the saints and the beloved city, but fire
> came down from heaven and consumed them, and the devil
> who had deceived them was thrown into the lake of fire and
> sulfur where the beast and the false prophet were, and they
> will be tormented day and night forever and ever. Then I saw

a great white throne and him who was seated on it. From his presence earth and sky fled away, and no place was found for them. And I saw the dead, great and small, standing before the throne, and books were opened. Then another book was opened, which is the book of life. And the dead were judged by what was written in the books, according to what they had done. And the sea gave up the dead who were in it, Death and Hades gave up the dead who were in them, and they were judged, each one of them, according to what they had done. Then Death and Hades were thrown into the lake of fire. This is the second death, the lake of fire. And if anyone's name was not found written in the book of life, he was thrown into the lake of fire (Rev. 20:7–15).

Because we have access to hundreds of pieces of the story of Scripture regarding God's judgment of the wicked, the use of fire imagery, and the appearance of actual fire, we can come to this passage in Revelation equipped to place these new concepts inside the overall story of God as revealed through the theme of *fire*. My understanding of what the author of Revelation is saying with the word picture of a lake of fire is shaped by and seen within the overall story of fire in Scripture. In short, for me it is another example of: Where God is, what is not of God is consumed.

Remember the importance of thematic repetition? Eternal conscious torment for unbelieving humanity is not a biblical theme. It is a doctrine created from a bad reading of one verse that has been removed from an incredibly rich story, spanning a thousand years of authors who have sought to express the reality of God's presence through their actual experiences with the fire of God's literal presence, and the thematic storytelling device of metaphor, often referring to God's activity toward the wicked as behaving like a consuming fire.

There are three more important observations:

1. Only Satan, the beast, and the false prophet are said to be tormented day and night forever and ever.
2. When humans march against the city of God, fire comes

from heaven and consumes them. This is consistent with
the majority of Scripture which speaks of an ending destiny
for the wicked—a blotting out, as if they never were. This
is also in tandem with the scriptural theme of human
authority. Who we choose to stand with, submit to, and
give our worship to ties us to the destiny of that particular
principality, that god, that power.

3. When those not found in the Book of Life are thrown into
the lake of fire, there is no description of torment day and
night forever and ever.

What does this data mean? You have to decide for yourself. I would say that
because the Bible is a story, the dogmatic conviction that hell is a lake of fire that
exists as a place separate from God would be quite a twist in the story of *fire*, and
the first time such a concept would be introduced.

I believe Scripture communicates to us that there is no place where God
is not. His very presence is perfect life and love. And the more this presence is
manifest or unveiled to creation, the greater the conflict between what is God
and what is not God, what is love and what is not love, what is life and what is
death. I believe it is reasonable to see this part of Scripture, which is attempting
to describe the revelation perspective of what will happen when there is no
separation left between the glory and holiness of God and the brokenness of
humanity, as a day of reckoning. What is not God, including death and Hades, is
consumed, utterly annihilated.

The overwhelming data of Scripture, if one wanted to make a conclusion as
to the destiny of the wicked, would be that God consumes them—utterly destroys
them—and makes it as if they had never existed. To ignore the entire story and
allow one reference in a heavily metaphoric, prophetic piece of apocalyptic
literature (also read: literature of the oppressed) is simply lazy exegesis and
intellectually dishonest theology. I believe it is a biblically weak assertion that is
discordant with the overwhelming scriptural theme of God's everlasting love to
create a doctrine that God would allow those he loves to exist forever in torment.

But you read Scripture cover to cover. Collect the data, and use the tools of
observation, story, thematic repetition. and author intent. Don't be afraid of the

unresolved. You have the power and the responsibility to decide for yourself.

CHAPTER 7

NAMING

When we adopted our second daughter twelve years ago, I figured eight kids was enough. However, life with Jesus is an adventure, and you never know what is around the next corner. One day, when my youngest daughter was three, we met a young lady named Cori. She had recently been discharged from our town's substance abuse treatment center, she was depressed and sometimes suicidal, and had recently become homeless. My wife and I invited this young lady to come live with us until she found her footing.

Cori is brilliant. Her wit is precise, engaging, and hysterical. She quickly warmed up to our tribe and began what would become intimate sibling relationships. After a few months in our home I would catch her looking wistfully at our multitude of family photos. (We had decided at the beginning of our adventure into adoption that we would take lots of photos and display them prominently around our house to help the new family members see their place and history every day on the walls and end tables of their home.) It wasn't long before Cori came to us and told us she didn't have a family. She wondered if we would want her as part of ours.

Now, Cori was not a minor. She was an adult young woman. We could see that she felt lost. Her drug usage, depression, and poor self-image screamed, "I'm all alone!" We had already fallen in love with her, and it was an easy decision to invite her to become a Sandler. However, we cautioned Cori to take some time and make sure that she wanted a new name. "After all," I told her, "Sandler's do specific things. We value what God values, and we live through our faith in Jesus."

Cori took some time to think about this big decision. One day a few weeks later, she was driving in town, discussing the matter with one of her friends on the phone. "Should I become a Sandler? Maybe I should hold on to my old name." Back and forth the conversation went, until in a moment of clarity, Cori shouted into the phone, "That's it. I'm gonna do it!" At that very moment, a police cruiser directly behind her turned on its lights.

As Cori pulled to the curb, she was petrified. You see, she had moved to Montana from California, where she had several unpaid tickets and a suspended license. Now, because Cori had become an integral part of our household and we had so many activities, she sometimes drove my other kids around town and we had put her on our family insurance policy. Thus, there were two names on the insurance card: Cori Baker and Dan Sandler. But there was only one name on the suspended driver's license: Cori Baker.

As she handed the officer her license, registration, and insurance, she had thoughts of hitting the gas and trying to outrun the police officer. She had a sense of dread as she pictured herself getting into the back of the police cruiser in handcuffs. She was sure her car would be impounded. As the officer returned to her car, she braced herself for the worst. He smiled, handed her back her documents and a written warning, and said, "Drive safe. You might want to get your taillight fixed."

My daughter was stunned. She stared at the warning she had been given and after a few seconds realized that the name on the warning was all wrong. The officer had run the name Cori Sandler, somehow combining my name from the insurance card and my daughter's name from the driver's license. Of course Cori Sandler had a clean driving record—she didn't exist . . . *yet*.

When I got home from work, my "new" daughter told me her story. We smiled and hugged each other through tears as we let the reality of our new, soon-to-be-permanent relationship sink in. Then I smiled at her and said, "You're a Sandler now. Pay your speeding tickets. That's what Sandlers do."

My daughter had a new name, and it was more than just a label, it was an identity. It was important. Cultures the world over place a great deal of meaning in naming of offspring, and this has been the case for thousands of years, and was perhaps even more so when the Hebrew Scriptures were written. Let's start to read our Bibles from the beginning, implementing the tool of observation, acknowledging the power of story, living with the unresolved, seeing the importance of thematic repetition and searching for the heart of the author's intent, and take a fresh look at some well-known passages of Scripture, keeping this idea of the importance of names in mind.

One of the interesting details of Scripture that tells us something of how the Bible works is the author's insertion of the name of God (*YHWH* as transliterated from Hebrew texts, or *I Am Who I Am* in English) into the story well before God reveals his name to Moses in the book of Exodus. In other words, the author, knowing the name of God, used this name liberally throughout the story before the point in the story where Moses first learns the name of God. The pre-Israel part of the story is told from the perspective of the people of Israel looking back to the time and place where their God began their story. And their story begins with creation.

There are hundreds of themes that thread their way through the many books that make up the Bible. One of the first themes, introduced to us in the creation story in Genesis, is one I will refer to as *naming*.

In the first chapter we see the Creator naming the parts of creation. As is the case in many cultures today, in ancient Semitic culture, naming was more than giving a label to an object to distinguish it from another object

The text of Genesis 2 also provides a piece of data that I have rarely heard presented in the conversation concerning male and female identities and roles in the church. The author chose to use the Hebrew word ezer, which is a derivative of the Hebrew word azar. This word represents the concept of one who gives aid by surrounding or protecting. This Hebrew word is used numerous times throughout the Bible to describe the activity of God's Spirit giving aid to humans. I believe it is an honest rendering of this Hebrew term to translate ezer as "a powerful force standing face-to-face." How did ezer, translated "suitable helper" in our English Bibles, come to mean the plumber's assistant? Woman submits to man. Woman cannot teach man. Woman cannot have authority over a man. Woman cannot, cannot, cannot...

for identification purposes. Rather, naming was the actual act of imbuing a thing with identity. What God *named* something was what it became and how it functioned.

In Genesis 1, the first Hebrew word translated *Adam* in our English Bible is also sometimes translated *man*. Did you know this Hebrew concept includes both a *feminine and a masculine* aspect? It is misleading to treat the translation of this Hebrew concept by moving back and forth between *Adam* and *man*, even though the Hebrew word is the same. It is also misleading to use the English concept of *man* as though it is a synonym for the Hebrew word *aw-dawm* (English *Adam*). Because this Hebrew term can include both male and female, it would be more accurately rendered *human*. It is not until after the rib, or "side," is taken out of the *aw-dawm* or *human* that we get a Hebrew word that means "man"—*eesh*—which is specifically masculine.

Why is this important? Because every empowering, naming statement that God makes about the *aw-dawm* he has created is made over humankind, not man exclusively. In many denominations and churches, to refer to God with anything other than the male pronoun is sacrilege, but in Genesis 1:26–27, God declares, "Let us make the *aw-dawm* in our image," and then creates the *aw-dawm*: "male and female he created them." If we reflect God's image as males and females, does that mean God's nature is the source of attributes that we see expressed through both male and female humanity? And if this idea is faithful to the data of Genesis 1 and 2, why is God referred to exclusively as male for the rest of the Bible story? All the way down through history, society has reinforced this male-only concept of God. However, after extensive and careful observation of the text, it would seem that the image of God is expressed uniquely through both men and women, requiring us to reconsider our male-only understanding of God.

God's creative intent was to make a being like himself/herself, and so God made a being that was both male and female. God then gave both parts of this expression of his/her likeness the Great Commissioning of multiplying, filling, ruling, and subduing the earth. When the *aw-dawm* partners with God and names the animals, co-creating with God, this is both the maleness and femaleness of God's image and likeness working in concert.

Why do I make this observation about the data of the text? There is only one place in Scripture where the story, as it unfolds, is devoid of any sin. There is a season in human history where everything functioned as God intended it. It could have been many days, years, centuries, or millennia. There is no indication in the text as to how long humankind existed in a perfect creation without sin in the story. Imagine thousands of years—the maleness and femaleness of God in human flesh living in harmony. Powerful, whole, creative, intimate beings, functioning as they were created to function, side by side.

The text of Genesis 2 also provides a piece of data that I have rarely heard presented in the conversation concerning male and female identities and roles in the church. The author chose to use the Hebrew word *ezer*, which is a derivative of the Hebrew word *azar*. This word represents the concept of one who gives aid by surrounding or protecting. This Hebrew word is used numerous times throughout the Bible to describe the activity of God's Spirit giving aid to humans. I believe it is an honest rendering of this Hebrew term to translate *ezer* as "a powerful force standing face-to-face." How did *ezer*, translated "suitable helper" in our English Bibles, come to mean the plumber's assistant? Woman submits to man. Woman cannot teach man. Woman cannot have authority over a man. Woman cannot, cannot, cannot . . .

The data of Genesis 2 is relatively clear: Man and woman were separated from one unified whole. The author of Genesis indicates that it is an expression of the likeness and image of God in humanity when the two become one flesh and live in harmony—honoring, promoting, serving, submitting, and empowering one another. It is my contention that this part of the story is what God intended. The rest of Scripture tells us the effect of humankind grasping for something other than God's heart, which should be identified as an aberration. What we have made of the original creation, as people entangled with sin, is not God's heart. Part of the story that tells what humanity is dealing with as a result of our divorce from God's creative intent is what I call Sin Management Scripture, and it should be viewed as temporary, incomplete, and sometimes even inaccurate. This type of interpretation is vastly different from the Scripture that reveals God's heart for us. What has happened as a result of humanity separating ourselves from our Creator should never supplant God's creative intention.

But showing the coexistence of masculine and feminine is not all we see when observing naming in Genesis. Adam participates and *names* the animals God had created. We also see that Adam names the one God has fashioned from his rib. I believe it is a fair observation of the text that God and then-humanity, who was created in God's likeness and image, are creating together as they name things. God fashioned us in his/her image, and the one fashioned in God's likeness imbued parts of creation with identity, naming, calling out, and proclaiming its worth and function in God's creation.

If we observe this theme of naming as the story of Genesis continues, we notice several noteworthy events that might not otherwise be detected. In the fifth chapter, Lamech has decided to name his son Noah (which means *rest*) and adds that: "Out of the ground that the LORD has cursed, this one shall bring us relief from our work and from the painful toil of our hands" (Gen. 5:29).

The rest of Scripture tells us the effect of humankind grasping for something other than God's heart, which should be identified as an aberration. What we have made of the original creation, as people entangled with sin, is not God's heart. Part of the story that tells what humanity is dealing with as a result of our divorce from God's creative intent is what I call Sin Management Scripture, and it should be viewed as temporary, incomplete, and sometimes even inaccurate.

Did you catch that? Lamech decides to create by naming. He *names* his son Rest, and the author emphasizes the significance by adding Lamech's explanations of its importance. Lamech is creating a solution to the curse on the ground that was declared in chapter 3. He desires rest from this painful toil, so he *names* his son. Does Lamech have this kind of authority? Is it his place to name and create a solution to this divine pronouncement of toil and struggle? Let's let the text answer this question.

In chapter 8, verse 21, the author reports God's promise, "I will never again curse the ground because of man." This is the first thing the Creator says following the end of the flood, the disembarking from the ark, and the consequent sacrifice. This is the Creator's response to Rest's (Noah's) successful completion of his assignment to survive the flood in an ark with his family and all those animals the first humans helped create. I would propose that this statement by God, to never again curse the ground, put in this position in the story, resolves our question concerning Lamech's naming of his son.

So here is my question: Does the text point to an image bearer, a like-God being, with the authority to rule and subdue the earth? How should we take this data? I would suggest that the text of Scripture tells a story of a man (Lamech) naming—creating identity and purpose—his son. And that this creative, naming act successfully exercises authority over the earth that he (humankind) was specifically created to rule and subdue.

There is much we can learn by observing the story of Noah. As Noah and his family leave the ark and step onto the earth again, the author uses language that points to a theme of recreation. He references many of the words and phrases from Genesis 1:

> And God blessed Noah and his sons and said to them, "Be fruitful and multiply and fill the earth. . . . every beast of the earth and upon every bird of the heavens, upon everything that creeps on the ground and all the fish of the sea. Into your hand they are delivered. Every moving thing that lives shall be food for you." (Gen. 9:2–3)

So here we are again. Humankind poised with the potential and amazing possibilities of God's creation. Still image-bearing. Still in his/her likeness. Still commissioned to rule and subdue, multiply and fill. Let's see what happens . . .

Once again, the theme of naming presents itself in a way that suggests creative authority. Noah's sons have been mentioned by name twice during the story of the flood. They are listed as Shem, Ham, and Japheth. It is interesting to heed the data at this point in the story. Before we learn anything about the actions of his sons, they are listed by name again:

> The sons of Noah who went forth from the ark were Shem,
> Ham, and Japheth. (Ham was the father of Canaan.) These
> three were the sons of Noah, and from these the people of the
> whole earth were dispersed. (Gen. 9:18–19)

An oddity of the text that might not at first seem significant is the identification of "Ham being the father of Canaan." Maybe an editor's note? Maybe a factoid of history mentioned in passing? Verse 22 again identifies Ham as the father of Canaan and notes an indiscretion of no small significance. Noah planted a vineyard and subsequently became drunk and lay "uncovered" in his tent. Ham then "saw the nakedness of his father." A good case can be made that Ham either observed a sexual encounter or participated in a sexual encounter with one or both parents. (But this is not my point so please don't get stuck on the naughty possibilities in the text.)

As in the story of the Garden, there is human nakedness and subsequent shame. In his anger? shame? embarrassment? Noah declares a curse over his son's progeny and speaks creative identity over his grandson. For a third time the name "Canaan" is used, when in verse 25 Noah declares, "Cursed be Canaan; a servant of servants shall he be to his brothers."

He also says,

> Blessed be the LORD, the God of Shem;
> and let Canaan be his servant.
> May God enlarge Japheth,
> and let him dwell in the tents of Shem,
> And let Canaan be his servant.

Naming! There it is again. What is Noah doing? What does Noah *think* he is doing? What is the effect? Does the narrative give Noah the authority to do what he does?

Canaan is not yet a player the story. Ham is the guilty party. I suggest to you that Noah is naming Ham's progeny. He is giving Ham's line identity and function. The name Canaan means *less than; to bend the knee; to humiliate, to vanquish; to bring down into subjection, make humble, demote, subdue.*[6]

Stay with me. It's hard to read the Bible without an expectation derived by bedrock presuppositions—those unexamined prethoughts. We see through a lens of ideas like *God is sovereign. He chooses whom to bless and whom to curse* (doesn't he?), *whom he loves and whom he hates* (Rom. 9:13, quoted from Mal. 1:2–3). His redemptive plan, his omnipotence, his omniscience, his perfect will—all of these theological assertions crowd in at this moment in a cacophony of "truth," making it almost impossible to see the direction the text is pointing.

What direction is that? Noah *named* his son's line *Less Than.*

Noah, in his anger, embarrassment, and offense, gave the identity of *demoted* to a large portion of humanity.

Later, as the descendants of Shem dispossess the descendants of Canaan, we might want to refer to this piece of data as we make theological decisions about God's favor, God's will, predestination, and election. Did Noah have the authority to name and create identity? Did his reaction to his sons' actions—cursing Ham's seed and naming his grandson *Less Than* or *Demoted*—have anything to do

> *Is it possible that all evil, all dysfunction inside of God's perfect creation, is a result of humanity refusing to be satisfied with the name our Creator has given us?*

with the trajectory of Ham's progeny, the people of Canaan? Did Noah's blessing of Shem and Japheth's progeny have anything to do with the future trajectory of their offspring?

Before you close this book and toss it on the pile with the other heretics, consider this. Nowhere in the text is there any other explanation as to the purpose and effect of this naming. Without importing concepts derived from other portions of Scripture (different authors with different purposes and themes), the text, on its own merits, points in a direction that challenges many mainstream building blocks of orthodoxy. Did God mean for Noah to name a portion of humanity *Less Than?* Was the Creator behind the scenes pulling the strings, determining this nasty turn of events for a great deal of those made in his image? Did God approve of this naming?

I don't know. I don't have to. What I do know is that this is the data before us. What will we do with it? Will we respect the text? Will we honor the author? Will we take the posture of one like a child, in humility, and head off in the direction indicated by the text without knowing where it will lead? Are we explorers, or are we policemen?

I understand that the numerous genealogies in Scripture are tedious at best, and we generally read them as connecting the different stories. Have you ever thought of *why* genealogies? Do you see all the names? Seen as part of the stories and not as isolated connecting pieces, we might just notice how much naming is going on. There is so much naming data in Genesis that I would suggest that this is one of the major characteristics of humankind being made in God's image. God has created, but so has humanity. Much that has happened and is happening in our world is attributed to God as Creator. Theological ideas like sovereignty, election, predestination, omnipotence, and omniscience serve to funnel all happenings in creation toward the "perfect will" of God. However, the data of Genesis points in a different direction. Humankind is powerful, capable of creating in our own right, shaping God's creation into our own image.

We see another example of this in the story of the Tower of Babel in Genesis 11. "Then they said, 'Come, let us build ourselves a city and a tower with its top in the heavens, and let us make a name for ourselves'" (Gen. 11:4).

Why does humanity insist on making a name for itself? We already have a name. Is it possible that all evil, all dysfunction inside of God's perfect creation, is a result of humanity refusing to be satisfied with the name our Creator has given us? Is it possible that the data of Genesis tells a story of humanity creating identities and realities on our own, apart from our Creator's heart for us? Is it possible that the data of Genesis tells a story of humanity being much more powerful than we have been taught?

My opinion is that human history is the sum total of the human will, not God's perfect will. We are powerful, individual creative agents inside the greater organism of humanity that governs creation. When we accept the name God gives us, we release his/her heart into creation. When we partner with any other name, we release the attributes of the one who whispered that lie into our hearts.

While I believe Christ-followers must reposition the importance of the authority and effect of human choices to name things with or without God's heart. I believe we have sorely confused how God interacts with humanity by ignoring the creative intent described and carried out in Genesis. I believe that the theologies that name humanity as small, unworthy, totally depraved, and insignificant next to the holiness and power of God ignore and pervert the name God has given us from the beginning. Yet, I would be remiss if I did not also assert that God knows what he is doing. However, there seems to be a clear connection between what God wants for creation and our decision to choose it.

I would also be remiss if I did not mention that I find the doctrine of sovereignty and its attendant ideas of God being in control and "allowing" evil to happen on the earth an intentional parting from the information in the text. It might make us feel better about things. It might make "sense" to us as we try to make sense of the world in which we live, but we do not find this doctrine in the pages of the text of Genesis. Mankind continues to name and exercise its authority to create, rule, and subdue. The only difference is there is now another motive in play separate from enjoying the love and intimacy for which we

> ... *human history is the sum total of the human will, not God's perfect will.*

were created. Thus, Lamech can bring relief from a curse, while Noah creates an entirely new curse. The narrative of Genesis positions humanity, made in the Creator's image, as a powerful force that stands face-to-face with God. Our choices matter. We co-create. This ability to create is like our Creator's powerful ability to create and is specifically given to humankind to name, shape, and steward.

I propose to you that God knew what he was doing when he made humanity in his (her!) likeness. I propose to you that God's creative intent was to have an intimate relationship—a partnership, even—with a being like himself.

I wonder if we could step back for a second and look at the practical realities of our theologies. If God created humanity in his image and likeness for the purpose of filling, ruling, and subduing the earth, and we fail to function as such, then God is a bumbling fool, creating ineffectively. However, because I believe God is good at his job, I expect that what he has intended will be accomplished.

This is how story works. There is tension, unresolved choices, pain, and chaos caused by the actions of the characters in the story. What will happen? Can God accomplish his purposes? How will he do this? Tune in next week for . . . *The Gospels.*

Remember that upstairs epiphany I had? The one that made me see prethought for what it was and question others' influences on the way I approached Scripture? It had to do with Noah too:

> To me this is like the days of Noah,
>> when I swore that the waters of Noah would never again cover
> the earth.
> So now I have sworn not to be angry with you,
>> never to rebuke you again.
> (Isa. 54:9 NIV)

What? God will never be angry with his people? God will never rebuke his people again? This is the best thing I had ever heard! This is truly good news! *Why had I never heard this before?* Just nine verses away is the most popular piece of Old Testament Scripture in my evangelical world, Isaiah 53. This Scripture I knew. I had heard hundreds of messages about the revelation of Jesus in verse 5:

> He was pierced for our transgressions,
> he was crushed for our iniquities;
> the punishment that brought us peace was on him,
> and by his wounds we are healed.

Remedies for our sin and brokenness—hallelujah! But a remedy for God's anger, his horrifying wrath, his disappointment, and disapproving gaze at my bad behavior?

> To me this is like the days of Noah,
>> when I swore that the waters of Noah would never again cover
> the earth.

So now I have sworn not to be angry with you,
never to rebuke you again.

This is what is commonly referred to in the study of Old Testament literary devices as a parallelism. Just as A, so is B. If A is a promise, then B is a promise. If A is for everyone, then could B possibly be for everyone? If A is forever . . .

Isaiah is telling us the story of his encounter with God and reporting to us what he believes God said to him. My translation of what God said to Isaiah is, "This thing I am telling you about, this amazing good news that one is coming who will take away the sin and brokenness of my children, it will change everything. This revelation is similar to the event Noah experienced. Humanity became convinced that the earth would never be destroyed in a flood again. Now I intend to convince you that I will never be angry with you again; I will never rebuke you again."

The concept in Hebrew translated into *rebuke* in our English Bibles carries the idea of rendering a correction that comes with disapproval. This disapproval is the equivalent of a mini-story telling us about our unworthiness. It isn't, "Hey, you spilled something. Let me help you clean it up." But rather, "Hey, you spilled something. Don't be so clumsy."

Isaiah is a prophet. He sees into the spiritual realm and reports what he sees. In this particular story he has seen a Redeemer repositioning the people of God in a relationship with God and his creation where sin and brokenness no longer define, or even affect, their identity. Chapter 53 is such good news. Consequently, preachers all over the globe have taught the gospel from this part of the story. Unfortunately for us, somebody in the distant past decided to put a chapter break in the most inconvenient spot. There is no indication that Isaiah is saying a new thing or that what he is seeing has changed to a new idea or a new timeline. Chapter 54 is part of the same revelation as chapter 53. Along with redemption (restored value) and healing (restored wholeness) comes restored identity.

Not only does Isaiah see God sending one to redeem and heal, Isaiah also sees this event restoring humanity to a relationship with their Creator that is not based on fear, anger, and unworthiness.

This of course begs the question as to why previous writers of Scripture told a story of fear, anger, and unworthiness. If Isaiah sees and reports to us that a Redeemer will take away our sin and heal us, and if this event will restore our ability to hear God's narrative about us, an identity that Isaiah specifically says will not contain anger or rebuke, we are left with a dangerously important question: Has God changed his nature, strategy, or posture toward humanity, *or* are we, as his image bearers, broken by our own rebellion, coming back into alignment with the truth about who God has always been and who he has always believed we are?

This is an important seminal question about how the Bible works. Is progressive revelation a concept describing our progress in returning to the truth about ourselves, or is progressive revelation a concept describing how God is *changing* how he relates to us?

... if the story of Scripture has progressed to this ultimate, perfect, powerful, complete revelation in Jesus, is it possible that we should view previous descriptions by scriptural authors about who God is and how he relates to us as incomplete and even inferior...

This question is scary, I know. It touches so much of how we have been taught the world, Scripture, and Christ-following works. But it is a question that we must face. We must decide.

If Jesus reveals the Father to us—"Whoever has seen me has seen the Father" (John 14:9); if Jesus is "The radiance of God's glory and the exact representation of his being" (Heb. 1:3 NIV); if the story of Scripture has progressed to this ultimate, perfect, powerful, complete revelation in Jesus, is it possible that we should view previous descriptions by scriptural authors about who God is and how he relates to us as incomplete and even inferior to the revelation that Isaiah sees as he writes about the one who is to come, one who will be pierced for our transgressions and crushed for our iniquities and whose time on this earth will forever change our understanding of how God thinks of us and how he desires to relate to us?

What if God has always loved us and desired to protect us from sin and its consequences? What if God has never been angry, despite the opinions of ancient men who described their God encounters through the lens of their understanding of how the heavenly realm worked? What if God is and has always been constantly revealing his love, his pursuit, his amazing heart to be with us, and we couldn't see it until we saw Jesus?

Now *that* is good news!

EPILOGUE

I am honored that you chose to journey through the pages of this book with me. For some, I know the path down into the valleys of the unknown and over the intimidating mountains of the status quo has been more difficult than for others. Some of the concepts I've described or the possible directions I've suggested may have rubbed you the wrong way. Perhaps you strongly agreed with some of my various ideas and strongly disagreed with others. Others of you might be frustrated because you feel you now have more questions than when you began. What you thought to be resolved, certain, and rigid about who you are and what you believe might have shifted, leaving you with a sense of the unresolved and a greater awareness that there might be more. Hope, courage, and the invitation to explore may produce in you a feeling that is uneasy—deeper questions, thoughts, and feelings that do not leave you feeling secure. Yet, I do not apologize for the discomfort this book may have caused, because I believe discomfort can be the catalyst for a deep engagement of the heart and mind.

One thing you might notice about our sense of comfort, safety, and identity is that God is always asking us why we feel comfortable and safe and on what or whom we base our identity. He is consistently provoking us to examine upon what these feelings and narratives are built. This is why there are such pervasive themes of trees, gardens, and seeds in Scripture. God is always speaking to his prophets, shepherds, teachers, and followers, encouraging them to examine the root, the place of origin, the source. Leading his people—Abraham, Jacob, Moses, the Israelites, David, and even Jesus—into the wilderness, the barren land, the place of questions, was designed to position them to either start over or allow their authentic connection to God to be tested. Was their sense of comfort, safety, and identity a product of trusting and believing that their God was the only source of life and love, or were they tragically willing to share that special place of intimacy, trust, and authority with someone or something else along the way?

God is not angry with us. He knows pain, betrayal, and cultural inertia can carry us away from his love. His constant invitation—that which we think of as revelation—beckons, even woos, his people toward his life, divine connection, and intimate love. These are the only true and permanent sources for comfort, safety, and identity.

My dream in writing this book for you was to draw you into this place of the unknown, to cause you to reexamine not only how you approach the Bible, but what you have decided it says, ultimately rebuilding your faith with these tools: observation, living in the unresolved, valuing the place of story, attention to themes and their repetition, and a tenacious habit of always looking for the author's intent. I believe it is in this place of humility and openness, courageously taking responsibility for what we choose to believe to be God's heart for us and this world, that God will reveal himself to us.

I realize it may seem daunting, this overhaul of the metanarrative from which we live, think, and make our choices. Changing the way we approach something that we have held sacred for years, and that may have been passed down for generations, is not a simple thing. You may have no idea where to begin.

Use the themes of seeds, planting, seasons, and harvest as your guide. Prepare the soil of your heart in time alone with God spent in prayer and worship. Commit to being open to what God has for you, even if it challenges that which you once held absolute. Once you have done this, begin to read and study entire books of the Bible at a time. In the absence of a strong leading to a particular book, I suggest starting in Genesis and working your way through the Bible. Observe everything you can. Train your eye to look for the repetition of words, phrases, concepts and themes. Invest the time to learn about each author's worldviews—the ways in which the people of his day thought and the values they followed—all the while asking yourself what his original intent was. Feel the rhythm and power of the story, moving your perspective around to observe the different characters in the narrative. Pay attention to the storytelling devices the author is using. Don't be afraid to ask questions! Question again, and again, and again. And if you can't find the answer, give yourself permission to rest and wait in the unresolved for a season.

Trust that your Father wants what is best for you, and as you seek his Truth with a sincere heart, he will meet you in that small, quiet place. He wants to be known by his children. He delights in our curiosity and questions. Do not be afraid of this journey. God is more eager than we are for us to know him. As he did for his people before, he will guide you to his promises, even if it takes a cloud by day and a pillar of fire by night.

The greatest story ever told is waiting for you. It deserves to be read again, as if for the first time.

1   *Merriam-Webster.com, s.v.* "data," accessed January 1, 2018, https://www. merriam-webster.com/dictionary/data

2   H. M. Tomlinson, *Out of Soundings* (New York: Harper and Brothers Publishers, 1931)

3   *Dictionary.com, s.v.* "story," accessed January 1, 2018, http://www.dictionary. com/browse/story

4   These are excellent resources with much useful scholarship on the different types of literature; however, they will assume much of what my book asks us to reexamine: Robert Plummer, *40 Questions About Interpreting the Bible* (Grand Rapids, MI: Kreger Publications, 2010); Walter C. Kaiser Jr., *Introduction to Biblical Hermeneutics: The Search for Meaning* (Grand Rapids, MI: Zondervan, 1994, 2007); Sinclair B. Ferguson, *From the Mouth of God* (East Peoria, IL: Banner of Truth, 2014).

5   Thomas Cahill, N. T. Wright, Eli Lizorkin-Eyzenberg, and Josephus have been wonderful sources of culture and context for my journey through Scripture and church history.

6   James Strong, Strong's Expanded Exhaustive Concordance of the Bible (Nashville: Thomas Nelson, 2009), *s.v.* "offering."